LEARN SPANISH FOR BEGINNERS

Speak Spanish In 30 Days With Short Stories and a lot of Lessons

Romero de la Ossa

Table of Contents

CHAPTER 1: LEARNING STRATEGIES

HOW TO LEARN SPANISH QUICKLY AND EASILY

Acquiring a new language requires time, effort, dedication, and willpower. To learn Spanish quickly and easily, you will have to take advantage of available resources, tools, and opportunities to optimize your study time. Successful language learners use the following strategies to learn Spanish in a short span of time:

Allot a specific time every day for language training.

Consistently studying at a specific time each day will help build your study habits. In addition, it can help accelerate learning time by eliminating the need to relearn or re-acquire language skills that could have been easily forgotten due to prolonged intervals in learning sessions.

Learn the most important words in Spanish.

The most important words in Spanish are those that are commonly used in regular or day to day conversations. By learning and mastering these words, you will be able to communicate in record time. Strive to memorize at least 20 important words a day and you will be able to build a strong vocabulary in less than two months.

Learn Spanish-English cognates.

English, Spanish, and other Romance languages share thousands of common words. These are words that have identical spelling and meaning in both languages. Most cognates will have different pronunciation but learning them can help you build a large vocabulary overnight.

Speak the language and interact with Spanish speakers on a daily basis.

Interacting with Spanish speakers on a daily basis helps you hone your listening, reading, writing, and speaking skills. Nowadays, the internet facilitates communication between people from different parts of the world. It is also a valuable resource for obtaining video and audio files that you can use to enhance your listening skills.

Learn to sound like a native speaker.

Acquiring the accent, intonation, pronunciation, and other peculiarities of Spanish will require regular practice, repetition, and advanced listening skills.

Establish specific, measurable, achievable, relevant, and time-bound goals.

As soon as you have committed yourself to learn Spanish, you must establish daily, weekly, and monthly goals that will motivate you and serve as your yardstick for evaluating your progress.

CHAPTER 2: THE FUNDAMENTALS OF SPANISH

THE SPANISH ALPHABET

The alphabet is the building block of a language. By learning the Spanish alphabet, you will gain an understanding of the uniqueness of this language. The Spanish alphabet uses the Latin or Roman alphabet and the same 26 letters found in the English alphabet. In addition, it uses 'ñ', a letter which has come to be associated with the language. The letters Kk and Ww were added to the original alphabet to accommodate words of foreign origin.

Here is the Spanish alphabet, their letter names, and sound:

Letters	Name	Pronunciation
A a	a	ah
B b	be	bay
C c	ce	say
D d	de	day
E e	e	ay
F f	efe	effay
G g	ge	hay
H h	hache	ah-chay
I i	i	ee
J j	jota	hotah
K k	ka	kah
L l	ele	el-lay
M m	eme	em-ma y
N n	ene	en-nay
Ñ ñ	eñe	en-yay
O o	o	ooh
P p	pe	pay
Q q	cu	coo
R r	erre	air-ray
S s	ese	es-say
T t	te	tay
U u	u	oo

V v	uve	beh
W w	uve doble	bveh doh-bleh
X x	equis	ay-keys
Y y	I griega	ee-gree-ay-gah
Z z	zeta	say-tah

PRONUNCIATION

Proper pronunciation is an essential element of efficient communication. Since Spanish words are spelled according to how they are pronounced, accuracy has become even more important. Proper pronunciation involves familiarity with the pronunciation and sound of each letter and their combination, syllabication, and stress.

In English, vowel sounds may vary from one word to another. Spanish vowels are pronounced in the same manner and never vary from word to word. Except when placed after q or g, vowels are almost always voiced.

Letter	Pronunciation	Example
a	like "a" in father	papa (potato)
b	hard sound, no aspiration – like "b" in ball	ente (good)
	soft sound – lips don't touch like the English "v"	hablar (to speak)
c	hard sound before a, o, u – like the "c" in car	camino (path)
	soft sound before e and I – like "c" in cell; in Spain, like "th" in thick	cielo (sky)
d	hard sound: like the "d" in door after l, m, n or a pause	falda (skirt)
	soft sound: like the "th" sound in there	nada (nothing)
e	sounds close to the "a" in late but shorter and crisper	cereza (cherry)
f	like the "f" in fast	grifo (faucet)
g	hard g: before a, o, u, and n like the "g" in gas	entesi (slender)
	soft g: commonly occurs when 'g' is found between vowels	agua (water)
	before e and i: like the "h" in hot but raspier	gente (people)
h	silent	la hora (hour)
i	like the "I" in machine	idioma (language)
j	the throaty English "h" in hack	viaje (trip)
k	like the "k" in kiss	kilómetro (kilometer)
l	like the "l" in mall	futbol (soccer)
ll	like the "y" in year	llamar (to call)
m	like the "m" in month	mano (hand)
n	like the "n" in net	nada (nothing)

o	like the "o" in no	poco (little)
p	like the "p" in pit but with no aspiration	perro (dog)
q	like the "k" in kitchen, always used with 'u'	aquí (here)
r	at the start of a word or after l, n, or s: trilled like RR	rico (rich)
	elsewhere – like the "dd" in ladder	ce ro (zero)
rr	trilled or vibrating sound, like saying "brr" with the tongue instead of the lips	perro (dog)
s	like the "s" in sit	ser (to be)
t	like the "t" in top but softer with no puff of air	triste (sad)
u	like the "u" in lunar	rubio (blond)
v	sounds like the Spanish "b" where the lips don't touch	avión (airplane)
w	like the "w" in wait, found in foreign words	ente (water)
x	in general, like the "x" in taxi	examen (exam)
	at the start of a word – like "ss" in kiss	xilófono (xylophone)
	like a throaty "h"	México (Mexico)
y	like "y" in yes	mayor (older)
	when used as a word or vowel, like the Spanish i	y (and)
z	like the "s" in supper, like "th" in thin in Spain	zapato (shoe)

Dipthongs

Diphthongs	Sound	Examples
au	like the 'ow' in bow	aunque (although)
ia	ya	piano (piano)
ai	eye	aire (air)
ei	like the 'ey' in hey	rey (king)
eu	close to 'eew'	entesi (neutral)
io	like 'yo' in yoyo	radio (radio)
iu	you	viuda (widow)
ue	like the 'we' in wet	fuego (fire)
oi	like the 'oy' in boy	hoy (today)

Syllabication

Syllabication Rules

Understanding how syllables are formed is a vital step to learning proper pronunciation in Spanish. It is important to know how to divide words into syllables as the letter combination generally determines proper pronunciation and use or placement of an orthographic accent.

Whenever possible, a syllable should end in a vowel. In many cases, a syllable consists of a consonant followed by a vowel:

niñani-ñayoung girl

casaca-sahouse

bodabo-dawedding

A consonant placed between two vowels forms a syllable with the second vowel:

oroo-rogold

acáa-cáhere

Two successive consonants will generally form two syllables in which the first consonant forms a syllable with the preceding vowel while the second consonant forms a syllable with the succeeding vowel.

Escuelaes-cue-laschool

bancoban-cobank

cantantecan-tan-tesinger

cuandocuan-dowhen

When there are three or more consecutive consonants, the first two will generally remain with the preceding vowel while the rest of the consonants will form a syllable with the succeeding vowel.

Conscienteconscien-teaware

panfletopan-fle-topamphlet

obstrucciónobs-truc-ciónobstructon, blockage

ombligoom-bli-gobelly button

entesimcon-stan-teconstant

entradaen-tra-daentry

Weak and Strong Vowels

Spanish vowels are either weak or strong and their classification as such has an impact on syllabication. The strong vowels are 'a', 'e', and 'o' and the weak vowels are 'i' and 'u'.

A Spanish syllable may only contain one strong vowel. A strong vowel placed beside one or more weak vowels may form one syllable together. Two adjacent weak vowels form a diphthong. Two adjacent strong vowels form two separate syllables.

Examples:

ciudadciu-dadcity

caerca-erto fall

toallato-a-llatowel

reinarei-naqueen

poetapo-e-tapoet

Some consonant combinations are not separated: br, ch, bl, cl, cr, dr, gr, gl, fl, fr, ll, pl, pr, qu, rr, and tr.

Bromabro-majoke

hablarha-blarto speak

carroca-rrocar

climacli-maclimate

clavecla-vekey

bicicletabi-ci-cle-tabicycle

trabajotra-ba-jojob

llamarlla-marto call

aplicara-pli-carto apply

hechohe-chofact

perrope-rrodog

frutafru-tafruit

gloriaglo-riaglory

pueblopue-blotown

siempresiem-prealways

frequentefre-quen-tefrequent

entesima-ma-ri-lloyellow

merengueme-ren-guemeringue

entesimcas-ti-llopalace

atrása-trásbehind

However, the combinations "rl," "sr", "tl", "nr", and "sl" form distinct syllables as follows:

islais-la island

perlaper-la pearl

atlasat-lasatlas

atlanticoat-lan-ti-coatlantic

A word's prefix forms a syllable of its own:

subliminalsub-li-mi-nal

desordendes-or-den

X is considered as two consecutive consonants when it takes the sound of ks.

Éxito ek-si-tosuccess

exámenek-sa-menexam

STRESS AND ACCENT MARK

Spanish uses one accent mark: the tilde or the acute accent. It is written above a vowel to indicate stress on a syllable. Spanish words are generally stressed on one syllable which may or may have a written accent.

Here are the most important rules on stress and accentuation:

The syllable with the accent mark receives the stress.

Víveres

cómo

pájaro

día

When a syllable does not contain an accented vowel, the following rules will determine the implicit location of the stress:

Words ending in n, s, or a vowel are stressed on the penultimate syllable.

Blanco**blan**-cowhite

roja**ro**-jared

nacionesna-**cio**-nescountries

bonitabo-**ni**-tapretty

casa**ca**-sahouse

Words ending in a consonant other than n or s are stressed on the final syllable.

Ciudadciu-**dad**city

papelpa-**pel**paper

relojre-**loj**watch

hablarhab-**lar**to speak

If the stress on a word violates the above rules, the word should have a tilde.

If a word ends in a vowel and the accent is on the final syllable, a tilde is required:

est**á**to be

If the consonant ending is other than –n or –s and the stress is on the penultimate syllable, it should have a tilde:

árbol_tree

az**ú**car_sugar

fácileasy

If a word is accented on a syllable other than the last or the penultimate syllable, a tilde is needed:

A-**mé**-ri-ca

In some cases, an accent mark is used to differentiate homonyms and monosyllabic words but has no effect on pronunciation:

sí (yes) si (if)

tú (you)tu (your)

él (he) el (the)

mí (me)mi (my)

dé (give)de (of, from)

té (tea)te (you, yourself)

más (more, most)mas (but)

sé (I know, be)se (himself, herself)

When an unaccented weak vowel forms a syllable with an adjacent strong vowel, the strong vowel receives the spoken stress.

Examples:

peruano

puede

An accented weak vowel placed beside a strong vowel form two distinct syllables:

biologíabio-lo-**gí**-abiology

policíapo-li-**cí**-apolice

Chapter 3: Numbers, Colors, Time, and Date

Cardinal Numbers

Counting and using numbers are important skills that you must learn in order to acquire other essential skills such as telling time and date and expressing quantity.

Spanish numbers are fairly easy to learn and can be mastered in less than two hours if you know the basic principles governing their formation.

It's important to memorize the numbers 1 to 19 as these are unique numbers. You will also need to remember the unique words for tens (veinte, treinta, cuarenta, noventa), hundreds (ciento,

doscientos, quininetos), and thousands (mil, dos mil). For the numbers 21 to 29, you will have to combine veinte (20) with the unit digit by first replacing its letter ending of 'e' to 'i' before affixing the unit digit. After treinta (30) and succeeding tens digits, you will simply combine the tens and units with the conjunction 'y' (and). Hence, thirty-two is treinta y dos, sixty-four is sesenta y cuatro, and ninety-nine is noventa y nueve.

When writing numbers in Spanish, take note that like most European languages, the comma and period are used inversely. That is, the comma is used to introduce the decimal numbers while the period is used to separate numbers by hundreds. For instance, to write 2,484,257.95 in Spanish, you will write 2.484.257,95.

Here are other important rules on cardinal numbers:

Uno

The number 'uno' (one) becomes 'un' when used before a masculine noun and 'una' when used before a feminine noun.

Examples:

un chicoone boy

un caballoone horse

una muchachaone girl

cuarenta y uno hombres forty-one men

setenta y una casasseventy-one houses

Cien/Ciento

The number ciento (100) is contracted to 'cien' when spoken, placed before a noun of whatever gender, or when used on its own. The longer form, 'ciento', is used when expressing large numbers except before 'mil' (thousand).

Examples:

cien casas 100 houses

cien hombres 100 men

cien mil casas100,000 houses

ciento cinco hombres105 men

The hundreds digits starting with two hundred have to change in form to agree with the gender of the noun they modify. This is true regardless of any intervening numbers between the hundreds digits and the noun they modify.

Examples:

doscientos carrostwo hundred cars

doscientas mesastwo hundred tables

doscientos cinco carrostwo hundred five cars

doscientas cuatro mesastwo hundred four tables

quinientos cinco librosfive hundred five books

0	cero
1	uno
2	dos
3	tres
4	cuatro
5	cinco
6	seis
7	siete
8	ocho
9	nueve
10	diez
11	once
12	doce
13	trece
14	catorce
15	quince
16	dieciséis
17	diecisiete
18	dieciocho
19	diecinueve
20	veinte
21	veintiuno
29	veintinueve
30	treinta
31	treinta y uno
39	treinta y nueve
40	cuarenta
41	cuarenta y uno
50	cincuenta
60	sesenta
70	setenta
80	ochenta
90	noventa
100	cien
102	ciento dos
182	ciento ochenta y dos
200	doscientos
201	doscientos uno
300	trescientos
500	quinientos
1000	un mil
2000	dos mil
1.000.000	un millón
1.000.000.000	mil millones
1.000.000.000.000	un billón

The Cardinal Numbers

ORDINAL NUMBERS

Ordinal numbers are used to indicate order, rank, or placement of a series of nouns. While each cardinal number corresponds to an ordinal number, only cardinal numbers from the first to the tenth are commonly used in Spanish.

Cardinal numbers end in 'o' and like other adjectives with –o ending, they have four forms to modify a noun as to gender and number. Hence:

Masculine Singular-oprimero

Masculine Plural-osprimeros

Feminine Singular-aprimera

Feminine Plural-asprimeras

When used before singular masculine nouns, primero and tercero have to take a shortened form:

el primer añothe first year

el tercer añothe third year

Ordinal numbers are generally used before a noun. However, when they are used to refer to a pope, a street, or royalty, ordinal numbers should be placed after the noun.

El papa Juan Pablo IIPope John Paul II

el papa Benedicto DecimosextoPope Benedict XVI

Carlos QuintoCarlos V

Isabel SegundaIsabel II

la Calle Sextathe Sixth Street

Ordinal numbers are generally used only up to the tenth (decimo). After this, you will need to use cardinal numbers.

For example, when stating the century:

the nineteenth century el siglo diecinueve

the twenty-first century el siglo veintiuno

To learn ordinal number quickly and easily, you will need to memorize the numbers from the first to the twelfth as there are all unique numbers. When you reach 13th to 19th, you will need to drop any written accent in the tens and attach it to the ordinal number from third to ninth.

Examples:

13th – décimo+tercerodecimotercero

16th - décimo+sextodecimosexto

19th – décimo+noveno decimonoveno

This pattern, however, does not apply to the ordinal number 18th as this would result to consecutive letter 'o'. Thus, eighteenth is written as decimoctavo.

From 21st to the 99th, you will need to remember the words for the multiples of ten and write it as a separate word. In the process, the ordinal number maintains its written accent.

For example:

21st vigésimo primero

31st trigésimo primero

99th nonagésimo entes

Abbreviating ordinal numbers

When describing nouns, you may want to abbreviate ordinal numbers. To do this, you will just have to add a decimal after the numeral and the superscript 'o' for most nouns, 'a' for feminine nouns, and 'er' for shortened forms primer and tercer.

Examples:

1st primer 1er

3rd tercer 3er

2nd entesi 2o

2nd segunda 2a

The Ordinal Numbers

first	primero
second	segundo
third	tercero
fourth	cuarto
fifth	quinto
sixth	sexto
seventh	septimo
eighth	octavo
ninth	noveno
tenth	decimo
11th	undecimo
12th	duodecimo
13th	decimotercero
14th	decimocuarto
15th	decimoquinto
16th	decimosexto

17th	decimoséptimo
18th	decimoctavo
19th	decimonoveno
20th	vigésimo
21st	vigésimo primero
22nd	vigésimo segundo
23rd	vigésimo tercero
24th	vigésimo cuarto
25th	vigésimo quinto
26th	vigésimo sexto
27th	vigésimo séptimo
28th	vigésimoctavo
29th	vigésimo noveno
30th	trigésimo
31st	trigésimo primero
32nd	trigésimo segundo
33rd	trigésimo tercero
34th	trigésimo cuarto
35th	trigésimo quinto
36th	trigésimo sexto
37th	trigésimo séptimo
38th	trigésimo octavo
39th	trigésimo noveno
40th	cuadragésimo
41st	cuadragésimo primero
50th	quincuagésimo
60th	sexagésimo
70th	septuagésimo
80th	octogésimo
90th	nonagésimo
100th	centésimo
200th	ducentésimo
300th	tricentésimo
400th	cuadringentésimo

500th	quingentésimo
600th	sexcentésimo
700th	septingentésimo
800th	octingésimo
900th	noningentésimo
1,000th	milésimo
2,000th	dosmilésimo
3,000th	tresmilésimo
4,000th	cuatromilésimo

FRACTIONS (FRACCIONES)

Fractions express quantity of a part of a whole.

The fractions la or una mitad (1/2) and el or un tercio (1/3) have distinct forms in Spanish:

la mitad/un medioone-half½

un tercioone-third1/3

dos terciostwo-thirds2/3

For the rest of the fractions, you will use a cardinal number as numerator and an ordinal number as denominator:

un cuartoone-fourth¼

un quintoone-fifth1/5

un séptimoone-seventh1/7

un novenoone-ninth1/9

tres cuartosthree-fourths¾

un centesimo one-hundredth1/100

DECIMALS AND PERCENTAGES

Parts of a whole may be expressed in decimal or percentages.

Percentage phrases are classified as masculine and are modified by a masculine article. For example:

El cincuenta por ciento de los matrimonios tiene éxito.

(Fifty percent of marriages are successful.)

In most Spanish-speaking countries, commas and periods are used inversely when writing numbers. Countries such as Mexico, Puerto Rico, and most parts of Central America follow the standard English usage.

Decimals are commonly expressed digit by digit when spoken. In Spain, you would say dos coma cinco cuatro (2,54). In other Spanish-speaking regions, you would say dos punto cinco cuatro (2.54).

COLORS

Colors are generally used as adjectives. Hence, most color names change their form to reflect the gender and number of the noun they modify.

Examples:

red apple|la manzana roja

red apples|las manzanas rojas

red car|el coche rojo

red cars|los coches rojos

Here are the exceptions:

Violeta (violet) is invariable.

Azul (blue), verde (green), and gris (gray) are invariable in gender but change in form to reflect the noun's number.

Here are the color names in Spanish:

amarillo	AH-mah-REE-yoh	yellow
azul	ah-SOOL	blue
naranja	nar-AHN-hah	orange
crema	krema	cream
café	kah-FAY	dark brown
dorado	do-rado	gold
gris	GREESS	gray
verde	BAYR-day	green
azul marino	a-SOOL ma-reeno	navy blue
rojo	ROH-hoh	red
rosa	ROH-sah	pink
púrpura	POOR-poor-ah	purple
marrón	mah-RON	brown
plateado	pla-te-ado	silver
violeta	vee-oh-LEH-tah	violet
blanco	BLAHN-koh	white
negro	NAY-groh	black

DAYS OF THE WEEK

The days of the week are never capitalized except when used at the beginning of a sentence. All days are masculine.

When a definite article is used before a day, it is translated as 'on'.

For example:

Hay una fiesta de cumpleaños el viernes.

There is a birthday party on Friday.

Mi padre no trabaja los domingos.

My father doesn't work on Sundays.

Take note that the days ending in –s retain their form in the plural. The article, however, must change to its plural form. Days that don't end in –s form the plural by adding s.

Examples:

el luneslos lunes

el miércoleslos miércoles

elsábadolos sabados

el domingolos domingos

Spanish	Pronunciation	English
lunes	*LOOH-nayss*	Monday
martes	*MAHR-tayss*	Tuesday
miércoles	*mee-AIR-coh-layss*	Wednesday
jueves	*WHAY-vayss*	Thursday
viernes	*vee-AIR-nayss*	Friday
sábado	*SAH-bah-doh*	Saturday
domingo	*doh-MEEN-goh*	Sunday

MONTHS OF THE YEAR

The months of the year are not capitalized except when used at the start of a sentence. Names for months are masculine.

Spanish	Pronunciation	Months
enero	eh-NEH-ro	January
febrero	feh-BREH-ro	February
marzo	MAR-zo	March
abril	ah-BRIL	April
mayo	MAY-o	May
junio	HOO-nio	June
julio	HOO-lio	July
agosto	ah-GO-sto	August
setiembre	se-TEE-YEM-bray	September
octubre	ok-TOO-brey	October
noviembre	no-VEE-YEM-bray	November
diciembre	dee-CEE-YEM-bray	December

SEASONS OF THE YEAR

Seasons of the year are not capitalized except when used at the start of a sentence.

verano	VEH-ra-no	Summer
primavera	pri-ma-VEH-rah	Spring
invierno	in-VYEH-no	Winter
otoño	OH-to-NYO	Autumn

TELLING TIME AND DATE

Knowing how to tell time and date are important skills that you can use on a daily basis.

To ask for time, you can say:

¿Qué hora es? What time is it"

To tell time in Spanish, you will use one of the feminine articles 'la' and 'las' to describe the 'hora' (hour), a feminine noun.

When the hour is at one o'clock' you will use the article 'la' with the verb 'es', the present tense third person singular form of the verb ser (to be).

To express all other hours, you will use the article 'las' and the verb 'son', the present tense third person plural form of 'ser'.

For example, to express the exact time, you will say:

Es la una.It's one o'clock.

Son las dos.It's two o'clock.

When the time is past the exact hour, you will express time by stating the minutes after the conjunction 'y' (and).

Examples:

9:25 Son las nueve y veinticinco.

It's twenty-five minutes past nine o'clock.

1:10Es la una y diez.

It's ten minutes past one.

When the time is a few minutes short of the exact hour, you can use 'menos' to express the number of minutes before the coming hour.

Examples:

9:45Son las diez menos quince.

It's 15 minutes before ten o'clock.

7:50Son las ocho menos diez.

It's 10 minutes before eight o'clock.

In addition, you can use media (half) to express the half hour and cuarto (quarter) to express the quarter.

2:30Son las dos y media.It's half past two.

4:15Son las cuatro y cuarto.It's a quarter past four.

3:45Son las cuatro menos cuarto.It's a quarter before four.

12:15Son las doce y cuarto.It's a quarter past 12 o'clock.

The expression a.m. and p.m. are not commonly used in Spanish regions. Instead, you can describe the time of day by adding 'de la tarde' (in the afternoon), "de la mañana" (in the morning), and "de la noche" (in the evening).

Examples:

Son las ocho y media de la mañana.

It's half past eight in the morning.

Son las tres de la tarde.

It's three o'clock in the afternoon.

Son las diez de la noche.

It's ten o'clock in the evening.

The 24-hour Clock

You can also use the 24-hour time, also known as military time, to express the hours.

Examples:

13:20 Son las trece veinte.It's 1:20 pm.

16:30 Son las dieciséis treinta.It's 4:30 pm.

Asking for and Telling the Date

To ask for the date, you can use one of these phrases:

What day is today?¿Qué día es hoy?

What is the date today?¿Cuál es la fecha de hoy?

What day is it today?¿A cuántos estamos hoy?

To tell the date in Spanish, use this pattern:

el + cardinal number + de + month + de + year.

Examples:

English Spanish

January 6, 2017el seis de enero de 2017

May 21, 1995el veintiuno de Mayo de 1995

December 25, 1945el veinticinco de diciembre de 1945

Take note, however, that you will use the ordinal number when expressing the date on the first day of the month.

Example:

Hoy es el primer día de febrero de 2017.

Today is the first day of February, 2017.

To express the date in full:

Hoy es viernes, el 13 de enero de 2017.

Today is Friday, the 13th day of January, 2017.

When writing the date in figures, you have to remember to place the date before the month and year:

Thus, January 13, 2017 is written as 13/01/2017.

Expressing the Year

To tell the year in Spanish, you will have to express it in the same way that you would express a regular number.

To express the year 2017 in Spanish, you would say 'dos mil diecisiete'. To express the year 1995, you would say mil novecientos noventa y cinco.

Expressing the Century

To express the century, you will use a cardinal number after the phrase 'el siglo':

the 20th centuryel siglo veinte

the 21st centuryel siglo veinte uno

CHAPTER 4: NOUNS AND ARTICLES

A noun is a word that names people, things, places, animals, ideas, and events. In Spanish, a noun's gender and number are important information that you will need to construct a grammatically sound sentence.

Unlike English, Spanish is a gender-specific language. Articles and adjective must agree with the noun or pronoun they modify both in gender and in number. Hence, there are usually four forms of modifier corresponding to the two genders and numbers.

ARTICLES

Spanish articles must match the gender and number of the noun they modify.

Definite Articles

There are four definite articles in Spanish and they all correspond to the English article 'the':

Gender	Singular	Plural
Masculine	el	los
Feminine	la	las

The definite article 'el' is used before a singular masculine noun while 'los' is used before a plural masculine noun.

Examples:

el chico (the boy)los chicos (the boys)

el gato (the male cat)los gatos (the male cats)

el coche (the car)los coches (the cars)

el libro (the book)los libros (the books)

The article 'la' is used before a singular feminine noun while 'las' is used before a plural feminine noun.

la chica (the girl)las chicas (the girls)

la gata (the female cat)las gatas (the female cats)

la mesa (the table)las mesas (the tables)

la ramita (the twig)las ramitas (the twigs)

Nouns of Mixed Genders

When modifying a group consisting of both masculine and feminine members, you will use the masculine article 'los' and the masculine form of the noun.

Examples:

los padres the parents

los hermanos the siblings

los perros male and female dogs

los gatosmale and female cats

Article Contraction

While contractions are quite common in English, there are only two instances of contractions in Spanish. They are required to ease pronunciation and both involve the masculine definite article 'el'.

When 'el' is used after the preposition 'a' (to), they contract and form 'al' (to the):

a +el = al

Iremos al mercado.We will go to the market.

Voy al hotel.I'm going to the hotel.

When 'el' is used after the preposition 'de' (of), they combine and form 'del' (of/from the):

de + el = del

¿Cuál es la comida del día? What is the meal of the day?

Es un empleado del hotel. He is an employee of the hotel.

Take note that no contraction is done when the article 'el' is part of the name of a city or country.

Examples: El Salvador, El Paso

Indefinite Articles

The indefinite articles 'a, 'an', and 'some' corresponds to four articles in Spanish:

Gender	Singular	Plural
Masculine	un	unos
Feminine	una	unas

Examples:

un chicoa boyunos chicossome boys

una chicaa girlunas chicas some girls

un gatoa catunos gatossome cats

un libroa bookunos librossome books

una mesaa tableunas mesassome tables

GENDER OF NOUNS

Spanish nouns are either masculine or feminine and they are modified by a corresponding article. When it concerns living creatures, grammatical gender generally follows natural gender. Hence:

MasculineFeminine

el hombre (man)la mujer (woman)

el hermano (brother) la hermana (sister)

el abuelo (grandfather)la abuela (grandmother)

el perro (male dog)la perra (female dog)

el gato (male cat)la gata (female cat)

el oso (male bear)la osa (female bear)

On the other hand, the grammatical gender of inanimate objects follows certain rules which must be learned in order for you to be able to construct accurate Spanish phrases or sentences. While it may take some time to memorize nouns and their gender, some gender rules or guidelines exist.

Nouns ending in 'o' are generally masculine

el campo field

el vestido dress

el cabellohair

el dedo finger

el cieloheaven, sky

el teatro theatre

el trabajo job

el dormitorio bedroom

el ojo eye

Nouns ending in 'a' are generally feminine

 la ramabranch

la hora time, hour

la manzana apple

la guitarra guitar

la rosa rose

la tumbatomb

la mesa table

la palabra word

la oficinaoffice

la piscina pool

la cama bed

Some nouns referring to occupations have similar forms for both genders and are only modified by the accompanying article.

MasculineFeminine

modelel modelo la modelo

judgeel juezla juez

poetel poetala poeta

bossel jefela jefe

soldierel soldado la soldado

managerel gerentela gerente

athleteel atleta la atleta

pianistel pianistala pianista

singerel cantantela cantante

astronautel astronautala astronauta

journalistel periodistala periodista

pilotel piloto la piloto

studentel estudiantela estudiante

Some occupations have slight difference in the endings for each gender:

teacherel maestrola maestra

doctorel doctorla doctora

bankerel banquerola banquera

waiterel meserola mesera

mail carrierel carterola cartera

presidentel presidente la presidenta

teacherel profesor la profesora

engineerel ingenierola ingeniera

Nouns ending in –ción, –sión, -dad, -umbre, ión, -ion, and –tud are feminine:

la dedicaciónthe dedication

la canción the song

la decision the decision

la soledadthe solitude

la ciudad the city

la legumbre the vegetable

la certidumbre certainty

la muchedumbrecrowd

la juventud the youth

la habitación bedroom

la estación station

la religion religion

la legion legion

la región region

la tension tension

Most nouns that end in –e, -l –r, -aje, or -or are masculine.

 el traje suit

el garaje garage

el perfume perfume

el maquillaje make-up

el personaje character

el paisaje landscape

el final end

el papel paper

el hotel hotel

el lugar place

el temor fear

el favor favor

el valor value

Nouns ending in –ma, -pa, or –ta which are usually words of Greek origin take on the masculine gender:

el programa program

el sistema system

el axioma axiom

el stigma stigma

el climathe climate

el mapamap

el tema topic, theme

el charisma charisma

el telegrama telegram

el dilemma dilemma

el fantasma ghost

el idioma language

el poema poem

el prisma prism

el cometa comet

el problema problem

el planeta the planet

Some nouns ending in 'o' are feminine while some nouns ending in 'a' are masculine.

Feminine nouns ending in –o:

la radiothe radio

la mano the hand

la polio polio

la fotothe photo

la moto the motorcycle

Masculine nouns ending in –a:

el díathe day

el cura the priest

el aroma fragrance

el sofá sofa

el tranvía tram

el panda panda

Names for months, days, oceans, seas, numbers, rivers, mountains, and compound nouns are generally masculine.

el mayo May

el martesTuesday

los cincuentafifty

el Océano Pacífico Pacific Ocean

el mar Báltico Baltic sea

el Monte Everest Mount Everest

los abrelatascan opener

Nouns ending in z are feminine:

la nariz nose

la voz voice

la nuez nut

la vejez old age

la paz peace

la faz face

la cruz cross

la luz light

la vez time

la validez validity

la raíz root

la rigidez rigidity

la actriz actress

la directriz directress

la emperatriz empress

Víctima and Persona

The nouns 'victima' and 'persona' are special feminine nouns that are invariable regardless of the gender of the person they refer to.

Mi madre es una persona agradable.

My mother is a nice person.

Mi padre es una persona valiente.

My father is a brave person.

La víctima murió en el camino al hospital.

The victim died on the way to the hospital.

FORMING PLURAL NOUNS

Spanish plural nouns generally end in –s or –es. You must learn some simple rules to determine which ending should be applied.

Nouns ending in é or in an unstressed vowel form the plural by adding –s:

el bebé (baby) los bebés (babies)

el chico (boy)los chicos (boys)

el padre (father)los padres (fathers)

el café (coffee)los cafés (coffees)

el hincapié (emphasis)los hincapiés (emphases)

la tribu (tribe)las tribus (tribes)

el sonido (sound)los sonidos (sounds)

la pera (pear)las peras (pears)

el juego (game)los juegos (games)

la bota (boot)las botas (boots)

el hermano (brother)los hermanos (brothers)

la casa (house)las casas (houses)

el vaso (glass)los vasos (glasses)

el color (color)los colores (colors)

la pluma (pen)las plumas (pens)

la cama (bed)las camas (beds)

la mesa(table)las mesas (tables)

el mono (monkey)los monos (monkeys)

la cosa (thing)las cosas (things)

la puerta (door)las puertas (doors)

Nouns ending in –y, a stressed vowel (á, í, ó, ú) other than é, and a consonant form the plural by adding –es:

el rey (king)los reyes (kings)

el borrador (eraser)los borradores (erasers)

la pared (wall) las paredes (walls)

el botón (button)los botones (buttons)

el león (lion) los leones (lions)

la majá (pestle)las majaes (pestles)

el maní (peanut)los maníes (peanuts)

el profesor (teacher)los profesores (teachers)

el mes (month) los meses (months)

la ciudad (city)las ciudades (cities)

el reloj (watch) los relojes (watches)

el autobús (bus)los autobuses (buses)

el país (country) los países (countries)

el papel (paper) los papeles (papers)

el bambú (bamboo) los bambúes(bamboos)

el tabú (taboo)los tabúes (taboos)

el jabalí (wild boar)los jabalíes (wild boars)

la universidad (university)las universidades (universities)

Exceptions:

Nouns ending in z form the plural by replacing z with c and adding –es:

el lapiz (pencil) los lápices (pencils)

la vez (time) las veces (times)

la actriz (actress) las actrices (actresses)

la voz (voice) las voces (voices)

la paz (peace)las paces (peace)

el avestruz (ostrich) los avestruces (ostriches)

el pez (fish)los peces (fishes)

el tapiz (tapestry) los tapices (tapestries)

la luz (light)las luces (lights)

Some nouns ending in –ión form the plural by dropping the written accent and adding –es:

la oración (sentence)las oraciones (sentences)

la conversación (conversation) las conversaciones (conversations)

la sección (section) las secciones (sections)

el avión (airplane)los aviones (airplanes)

la canción (song)las canciones (songs)

la televisión (television)las televisiones (televisions)

Some nouns ending in a stressed vowel other than é form the plural by adding –s:

el sofa (sofa) los sofas (sofas)

el menu (menu)los menus (menus)

la mama (mom)las mamas (moms)

el papa (dad)los papas (dads)

el champú (shampoo)los champús (shampoos)

Nouns ending in –c or –g form the plural by replacing –c with –qu or -g with –gu and adding –

es:

el frac (skirt)los fraques (skirts)

el zigzag (zigzag)los zigzagues (zigzags)

Some nouns have identical forms in the singular or plural and their number is determined by the accompanying appropriate article:

Nouns ending in –x have the same form for singular and plural

el fénix (phoenix)los fénix (phoenixes)

el tórax (thorax)los tórax (thoraces/thoraxes)

el bórax (borax)los borax (boraxes)

Nouns ending in –s have similar forms in the singular and plural if the final syllable is unstressed:

el atlas (atlas)los atlas (atlases)

el énfasis (emphasis)los énfasis (emphases) el

sacacorchos (corkscrew) los sacacorchos (corkscrews)

el análisis (analysis)los análisis (analyses)

el virus (virus) los virus (viruses)

el jueves (Thursday)los jueves (Thursdays)

Pluralia Tantum

These nouns are used dominantly or exclusively in the plural form:

los víveres supplies

los modales manners

los celosjealousy

las nupcias nuptials

las fauces jaws

los ambages hesitation

las afueras outside

los fastos chronicle

las gafas sunglasses

las cosquillas tickling

las albricias glad tidings

las pertenencias belongings

las pinzas pincers

los anales annals

las creces the increase

los gastos expenses

Some geographical names only take the plural form:

los Andes the Ands

los Alpes the Alps

las Antillas the Antilles

los Carpatos the Carpathians

las Baleares the Balearic Islands

las Azores the Azores

Some nouns can take on either the plural or singular form without changing their meaning:

la tijera, las tijeras scissors

la tenaza, las tenazas pincers

la enagua, las enaguas underskirt

el pantalon, los pantalones pants

la calza, las calzas stockings

SINGULARIA TANTUM

Some nouns are only used in the singular.

Nouns that designate unique phenomena and objects:

la luna moon

el sol sun

el horizonte horizon

el sur south

el norte north

Nouns that identify substances, products, and materials:

la lechemilk

el carbón coal

el trigo wheat

la mantequilla butter

el pan bread

Abstract nouns that identify state, action, or quality:

la alegría joy

el desarollo development

el orgullo proud

la valentía valor

Nouns that suggest total plurality:

la gente people

el dinero money

la ropa dress

Names of sciences as well as nouns ending in –ismo:

la medicina medical science

la ingenería engineering

el impresionismo impressionism

CHAPTER 5: PRONOUNS

A pronoun is a small word that you can use in place of a noun or noun phrase. Pronouns are usually classified according to their purpose or use in a sentence.

Personal pronouns represent specific people or objects. They can be the subject of a sentence or the object of a verb or preposition. Some are used to express possession.

SUBJECT PRONOUNS

Subject pronouns are personal pronouns that are used to refer to subject nouns. In English, you will always need a personal pronoun in place of a noun in a sentence or phrase. In Spanish, however, personal pronouns are not commonly used as the subject is generally identifiable through the verb's conjugation or ending.

Subject Pronouns

Singular	
I	yo
you – informal	tú
you –formal	usted, Ud.
he, she	él, ella
Plural	
We	nosotros (m), nosotras (f)
you all – informal	vosotros (m), vosotras (f)
you all – formal	ustedes, Uds.
They	ellos, ellas

Here are the most important features of Spanish subject pronouns:

yoThe pronoun 'yo' (I) is never capitalized expect when used at the start of a sentence.

tú, vosotrosThe pronoun tú is the informal or familiar form of 'you' and it is used when addressing close friends, relatives, children, or pets. Take note of the written accent which differentiates it from the possessive pronoun 'tu' (your). Vosotros is the plural informal form of 'you'.

usted, ustedesThe pronouns usted (singular) and ustedes (plural) are the formal forms of you in Spanish. You will use them to address older people, superiors, dignitaries, and other people you would normally want to address with formality.

DIRECT OBJECT PRONOUNS

A direct object pronoun takes the place of a noun used as a direct object. Here are the direct object pronouns in Spanish:

Singular	Direct Object Pronouns
me	me
You	te
him, her, it, you (formal)	lo, la
Plural	
Us	nos
you	os
them, you (formal)	los, las

Placement of Direct Object Pronouns

Direct object pronouns are placed before the conjugated verb or attached at the end of the infinitive or imperative forms of the verb.

Examples:

La quiero.I love her.

Lo vimos.We saw him.

Te conozco.I know you.

Nos llamaron.They called us.

Te conozco.I know you.

Lo tengo.I have it.

Las chicas **los** leen.The girls read them.

Los llamamos.We call them.

INDIRECT OBJECT PRONOUNS

An indirect object pronoun takes the place of a noun used as an indirect object. They indicate 'to whom' or 'for whom' an action is performed.

Here are the indirect object pronouns in Spanish:

Singular	Indirect Object Pronouns
to me, for me	me
to you, for you	te
to/for him, her, it, you (formal)	le
Plural	
to us, for us	nos
to you, for you	os
to/for them, you (formal)	les

Examples:

Su hermano **le** compró una casa.

His brother bought him a house.

Les dije un secreto.

I told them a secret.

POSSESSIVE PRONOUNS

A possessive pronoun is a word that takes the place of a noun modified by a possessive adjective. Possessive pronouns are used with a definite article and have four forms to indicate the gender and number of the noun they replace. They are the equivalent of the English possessive pronouns mine, ours, yours, his, hers, its, and theirs.

Here are the Spanish possessive pronouns:

	Masculine		Feminine	
Singular	Singular	Plural	Singular	Plural
mine	el mío	los míos	la mía	las mías
yours (familiar)	el tuyo	los tuyos	la tuya	las tuyas
his/hers/yours	el suyo	los suyos	la suya	las suyas
Plural				
ours	el nuestro	los nuestros	la nuestra	las nuestras
yours (familiar)	el vuestro	los vuestros	la vuestra	las vuestras
theirs/yours	el suyo	los suyos	la suya	las suyas

Este coche es el **mío**. This car is mine.

Estos coches son los **mios**. These cars are mine.

Su coche es mejor que el **mío**. Your car is better than mine.

Esa mesa es la **suya**. That table is hers.

Esas mesas son las **suyas**. Those tables are hers.

La pluma es la **vuestra**. The pen is yours.

Estas casas son las **nuestras**. These houses are ours.

Esta casa es la **nuestra**. This house is ours.

Interrogative Pronouns

Interrogative pronouns are words used for asking questions. An interrogative pronoun is commonly placed at the beginning or near the beginning of a sentence. Some Spanish pronouns have plural and singular forms and some have masculine and feminine forms to correspond with the number and gender of the noun they refer to.

The following are the interrogative pronouns in Spanish:

quién, quiénes (who, whom)

The pronoun quién is used to ask questions about people. Its plural form is quiénes.

¿Quién es el presidente de la clase?

Who is the president of the class?

¿Quiénes son sus amigos?

Who are your friends?

¿Para quien son estos regalos?

For whom are these gifts?

qué (what)

The pronoun qué is used to ask for information regarding the identification or definition of a thing or idea.

¿Qué pasa?What's happening?

¿Qué quiere usted?What do you want?

The phrases por qué and para qué are both commonly translated as "why". In this sense, por qué is the more commonly used phrase. Para qué is more commonly translated as "what for" and it is used to ask about the purpose or intent of something that occurred or is occurring.

¿Por qué estás aquí?Why are you here?

¿Por qué tiene miedo?Why is she afraid?

¿Para quien son estas manzanas?For whom are these apples?

cuál, cuáles (which one(s), what)

The use of cuál or cuáles generally conveys making a choice between two or more options. These pronouns are often translated as 'what'.

¿Cuál quieres – el pastel o el pan?

Which do you want – the cake or the bread?

¿Cuáles prefiere usted?

Which ones do you prefer?

cómo(how)

¿Cómo está usted?How are you?

¿Cómo te llamas?How do you call yourself?

cuánto, cuántos, cuánta, cuántas (how many, how much)

This interrogative pronoun has four forms to indicate the number and gender of the object or objects they refer to.

¿Cuántos coches tiene?

How many cars do you have?

¿Cuántas casas hay?

How many houses are there?

¿Cuánto azúcar está en esta taza?

How much sugar is in this cup?

dónde (where)

The interrative pronoun donde is used to ask about the location of a person or object.

¿Dónde vive usted?Where do you live?

¿Dónde está mi amiga?Where is my friend?

¿De dónde es Martha?From where is Martha?

If you want to ask "to where", you will use the form adónde:

¿Adónde vas? Where are you going?

Take note that interrogative pronouns are marked by a written accent to distinguish them from relative pronouns with similar spelling.

INDEFINITE PRONOUNS

Indefinite pronouns are words that stand for nonspecific person or thing. They are commonly used when making generalizations or when referring to no particular person or object. They may function as subject or object of the verb or preposition.

alguien (someone, somebody, anybody, anyone)

Alguien horneó un pastel ayer.

Someone baked a cake yesterday.

Alguien derramó la leche.

Someone spilled the milk.

algo (something, anything)

Algo provocó el ataque.Something provoked the attack.

Algo falló.Something failed.

alguno, alguna — one, a certain one

Hay muchos buenos cantantes aquí. Conozco alguno.

There are many good singers here. I know some.

algunos, algunas – some, a few (people or things)

Algunos están aquí solamente para pasar las horas.

Some are here only to pass the hours.

mucho, muchos, mucha, muchas – many, much

Muchos están satisfechos de su liderazgo.

Many are satisfied with his leadership.

cada uno, cada una – each one

Cada uno es un candidato para la graduación.

Each one is a candidate for graduation.

todo, toda – everything, all

Todo es como un sueño.

Everything is like a dream.

todos, todas – everyone, all

Todos están invitados a la fiesta.

Everyone is invited to the feast.

cualquiera - anybody, anyone, whoever

Cualquiera puede aprender a leer.

Anyone can learn to read.

otro, otros, otra, otras - another, another one, other one,

Uno da una pluma mientras el otro da un pedazo de papel.

One gives a pen while another gives a piece of paper.

uno, una, unos, unas —one, some

Unos no están interesados.

Some are not interested.

Una no está contento con su vida.

One is not satisfied with her life.

nada — nothing

Nada va a pararlo. Nothing is going to stop him.

nadie — nobody, no one

Nadie es perfecto. Nobody is perfect.

Nadie lo quiere. Nobody wants him.

ninguno, ninguna — nobody, none, no one

Ninguno va al banquete.Nobody is going to the banquet.

A double negative can occur when the negative pronouns nada, nadie, or ninguno are used after the verb as the part before the verb is generally formed as a negative.

Examples:

No veo nadie.I don't see anyone.

Él no tiene nada.He has nothing.

CHAPTER 6: VERBS

Verbs are words that denote an action or a condition. In Spanish, verbs change their ending, stem, or both to convey the person, mood, voice, and tense. This means that you can easily form a simple, one-word sentence with a single verb. This makes verb a very important part of speech. If you wish to express yourself properly in a short span of time, you must study a great number of commonly-used verbs and learn their endings in the different tenses and moods.

Verb Moods

Mood is a verb's property that indicates the speaker's perception of the action denoted by the verb. There are three verb moods in Spanish: indicativo (indicative), subjuntivo (subjunctive), and imperativo (imperative).

THE INDICATIVE MOOD

The indicative mood is the most commonly used mood in daily conversations. You will use it to express facts and reality in the present, past, and future.

There are 7 tenses in the indicative mood:

Present tense

Future tense

Imperfect tense

Preterite

Present perfect tense

Future perfect tense

Past perfect tense

CONJUGATING REGULAR VERBS

A verb may be regular or irregular. Regular verbs are those that form the past and future tenses in a predictable manner. A verb may be regular in some tenses and irregular in one or more tenses. There is no way to tell whether a verb is irregular or irregular at a glance. You need to learn the irregular ones as they are the most commonly used verbs in Spanish.

Regular verbs are grouped into three main categories according to their ending in the infinitive: AR verbs, ER verbs, and IR verbs. The classification is important as each verb group follows a unique pattern of conjugation.

To conjugate regular verbs in the present indicative tense, you must extract the stem of the infinitive by dropping the endings –ar, -er, or –ir.

Infinitives are verb forms which are not bound by time. Here are some examples:

hablarto talk

beberto drink

escribirto write

To obtain the stem you, you must drop the ending. Thus:

Infinitivestem and endingstem

hablarhabl + arhabl

beberbeb + erbeb

escribirescrib + irescrib

Once you have obtained the verb stem, you will need the applicable personal endings to properly conjugate the verb. Hence, the next step is to identify the subject. Once this is done, you will affix the prescribed ending for the verb according to its mood, tense, and subject.

THE PRESENT TENSE

The Spanish present tense verb form is equivalent to several tenses in English. For instance, 'como', the verb form of comer in the first person present indicative tense, may be used to convey the following meanings:

habitual actionI eat.

action in progressI am eating.

near future actionI will eat.

interrogativeDo I eat?

emphatic formI do eat.

past action continuing to the presentI have been eating.

Verb Chart

To express the present indicative tense, regular verbs should be conjugated using the following endings for each verb group:

Subject	-ar Verbs	-er Verbs	ir Verbs
yo	-o	-o	-o
tú	-as	-es	-es
él/ella/usted	-a	-e	-e
nosotros/nosotras	-amos	-emos	-imos
vosotros/vosotras	-áis	-éis	-ís
ellos/ellas/ustedes	-an	-en	-en

Take note that –er verbs and –ir verbs have similar endings for most subjects except for the first person plural and second person plural. In addition, the second person formal singular pronoun usted takes on the third person singular ending while its plural form ustedes takes on the third person plural ending.

Hence, when you conjugate the verbs hablar, comer, and escribir in the present indicative tense, you will have the following forms:

Subject	hablar (to speak)	comer (to eat)	escribir (to write)
yo	hablo	como	escribo
tú	hablas	comes	escribes
él/ella/usted	habla	come	escribe

nosotros/nosotras	hablamos	comemos	escribimos
vosotros/vosotras	habláis	coméis	escribís
ellos/ellas/ustedes	hablan	comen	escriben

STEM-CHANGING VERBS

Besides the change in their endings to reflect the person and number, some Spanish verbs change their stem in the present tense except in the first person and second person plural forms. In addition, except for –ir verbs which undergo stem changes in the preterite and present subjunctive, other verb groups generally do not change their stem in other tenses.

Verbs that change their stem from e to ie:

Here is how you will conjugate the verbs pensar, querer, and sentir in the present indicative tense:

	pensar	**querer**	**sentir**
	(to think)	(to want/love)	(to feel)
yo	pienso	quierdo	siento
tú	piensas	quieres	sientes
él/ella/usted	piensa	quiere	siente
nosotros/nosotras	pensamos	queremos	sentimos
vosotros/vosotras	pensáis	queries	sentís
ellos/ellas/ustedes	piensan	quieren	sienten

The following verbs change their stem in a similar manner:

atravesar to cross

calentarto heat

cerrar to close

comenzar to begin

despertarto awaken

empezarto begin

gobernarto govern

defender to defend

divertirto amuse

perder to lose

tropezar to stumble

advertir to warn, notify

convertir to convert

herir to injure

Verbs that change their stem from o to ue:

To conjugate the verbs encontrar, mover, and dormir, you'll have the following verb forms:

	encontrar	mover	dormir
	(to find)	(to move)	(to sleep)
yo	encuentro	muevo	duermo
tú	encuentras	mueves	duermes
él/ella/usted	encuentra	mueve	duerme
nosotros/nosotras	encontramos	movamos	dormimos
vosotros/vosotras	encontráis	mováis	dormís
ellos/ellas/ustedes	encuentran	muevan	duermen

The following verbs also fall under this group:

contarto count

almorzar to eat lunch

apostarto bet

costar to cost

encontrarto find

probar to try, prove

recordar to remember

rogar to beg

sonar to sound(sound)

soñar to dream

volar to fly

llover to rain

 volver to return

oler to smell

poder to be able

morir to die

IR verbs that change their stem from e to i when stressed:

To conjugate the verbs servir, repetir and medir:

	servir	repetir	medir
	(to serve)	(to repeat)	(to measure)
yo	sirvo	repito	mido

tú	sirves	repites	mides
él/ella/usted	sirve	repite	mide
nosotros/nosotras	servimos	repetimos	medimos
vosotros/vosotras	servís	repetís	medís
ellos/ellas/ustedes	sirven	repiten	miden

Here are the other –ir verbs that change their stem from e to i when stressed:

conseguirto get

competir to compete

corregir to correct

despedir to say goodbye

derretir to melt

elegir to elect

pedirto ask for

reír to laugh

seguir to follow, to tontinue

sonreír to smile

vestir to dress

The verb jugar changes its stem from u to ue:

yo	juego
tú	juegas
él/ella/usted	juega
nosotros/nosotras	jugamos
vosotros/vosotras	jugáis
ellos/ellas/ustedes	juegan

Verbs with irregular verb form in the first person singular

Some verbs have special forms in the first person singular.

Verbs that change from c > zc in the yo form:

	conocer	producir	aparecer
	(to know)	(to produce)	(to appear)
yo	conozco	produzco	aparezco
tú	conoces	produces	apareces
él/ella/usted	conoce	produce	aparece

			aparecemos
nosotros/nosotras	conocemos	producimos	
vosotros/vosotras	conocéis	producís	aparecéis
ellos/ellas/ustedes	conocen	producen	aparecen

This is generally true for verbs with –cer or –cir endings. Here are other verbs with special first person singular form:

agradecer to thank

amanecer to dawn

crecer to grow

establecer to establish

enflaquecerse to get thin

enriquecerse to get rich

nacerto be born

merecerto deserve

ofrecerto offer

obedecer to obey

permanecer to remain

padecer to suffer

parecer to seem

producir to produce

reducir to reduce

traducir to translate

conducir to drive, to conduct

The letter 'g' appears in the first person singular forms of some verbs:

caer (to fall)	caigo, caes, cae, caemos, caéis, caen
hacer (to do/make)	hago, haces, hace, hacemos, hacéis, hacen
traer (to bring)	traigo, traes, trae, traemos, traéis, traen
poner (to put)	pongo, pones, pone, ponemos, ponéis, ponen
valer (to be worth)	valgo, vales, vale, valemos, valéis, valen
tener (to have)	tengo, tienes, tiene, tenemos, tenéis, tienen

decir (to tell/say)	digo, dices, dice, decimos, decís, dicen
salir (to leave)	salgo, sales, sale, salimos, salís, salen
venir (to come)	vengo, vienes, viene, venimos, venís, vienen

Some verbs form their first person singular in a different manner:

	dar	caber	saber	ver
	(to give)	(to fit)	(to know)	(to see)
yo	doy	quepo	sé	veo
tú	das	cabes	sabes	ves
él/ella/usted	da	cabe	sabe	ve
nosotros/nosotras	damos	cabemos	sabemos	vemos
vosotros/vosotras	dais	cabéis	sabéis	veis
ellos/ellas/ustedes	dan	caben	saben	ven

Verbs which are accented on the final weak vowel

The weak vowels "i" and "u" form a dipthong when placed beside other vowels. To prevent them from forming a dipthong, a written accent is added to the last weak vowel. The accent is generally required when the weak vowels are stem vowels.

The following chart shows the conjugation for the verbs vaciar, continuar, and actuar:

	vaciar	continuar	actuar
	(to empty)	(to continue)	(to act)
yo	vacío	continúo	actúo
tú	vacías	continúas	actúas
él/ella/usted	vacía	continúa	actúa
nosotros/nosotras	vaciamos	continuamos	actuamos
vosotros/vosotras	vaciáis	continuáis	actuáis
ellos/ellas/ustedes	vacían	continúan	actúan

The following verbs likewise take a written accent on the weak vowel in the final syllable:

enviar to send

criar to raise or bring up

efectuar to bring about

confiar to trust

esquiar to ski

graduar to graduate

In most cases, however, the weak vowels are not stem vowels and must form a dipthong when placed beside another vowel.

Examples:

apreciar to appreciate

asociar to associate

anunciar to announce

divorciar to divorce

cambiar to change

copiar to copy

ensuciar to dirty

negociar to negociate

iniciar to initiate

estudiar to study

renunciar to renounce

limpiar to clean

Verbs ending in –uir

Verbs ending in –uir takes a 'y' in the indicative present tense ending whenever the 'i' is not found in the ending. Take note that this rule excludes verbs ending in –guir. The change takes places in all verb forms except for the first person plural and the second person plural.

Here are some examples:

	incluir	construir	contribuir
	(to include)	(to build)	(to contribute)
yo	incluyo	construyo	contribuyo
tú	incluyes	construyes	contribuyes
él/ella/usted	incluye	construye	contribuye
nosotros/nosotras	incluimos	construimos	contribuimos
vosotros/vosotras	incluís	construís	contribuís
ellos/ellas/ustedes	incluyen	construyen	contribuyen

	influir	huir	disminuir
	(to influence)	(to escape)	(to diminish)
yo	influyo	huyo	disminuyo
tú	influyes	huyes	disminuyes
él/ella/usted	influye	huye	disminuye
nosotros/nosotras	influimos	huimos	disminuimos
vosotros/vosotras	influís	huís	disminuís
ellos/ellas/ustedes	influyen	huyen	disminuyen

An orthographic or spelling change may occur to maintain the stress on the final stem consonant.

Verbs ending in –gir change from g to j when placed before 'a' or 'o':

	corregir	dirigir	exigir
	(to correct)	(to direct)	(to demand)
yo	corrijo	dirijo	exijo
tú	corriges	diriges	exiges
él/ella/usted	corrige	dirige	exige
nosotros/nosotras	corregimos	dirigimos	exigimos
vosotros/vosotras	corregís	dirigís	exigís
ellos/ellas/ustedes	corrigen	dirigen	exigen

	surgir	fingir	elegir
	(to arise)	(to pretend)	(to elect)
yo	surjo	finjo	elijo
tú	surges	finges	eliges
él/ella/usted	surge	finge	elige
nosotros/nosotras	surgimos	fingimos	elegimos
vosotros/vosotras	surgís	fingís	elegís
ellos/ellas/ustedes	surgen	fingen	eligen

Verbs ending in –guir drop 'u' in the first person singular when it precedes 'a' or 'o':

	conseguir	seguir	distinguir
	(to get)	(to follow)	(to distinguish)
yo	consigo	sigo	distingo
tú	consigues	segues	distingues
él/ella/usted	consigue	sigue	distinguee
nosotros/nosotras	conseguimos	seguimos	distinguimos
vosotros/vosotras	conseguís	seguís	distinguish
ellos/ellas/ustedes	consiguen	siguen	distinguen

SER AND ESTAR

The Spanish irregular verbs ser and estar both translate to the English verb 'to be' and are highly irregular in forms. Ser and estar are used differently and most Spanish learners encounter difficulties on their usage. Since both verbs are two of the most commonly used ones in Spanish, it is important to learn when one should be used over the other to be able to form accurate sentences.

Ser

The following chart shows the conjugation of the verb 'ser' in the simple tenses:

Subject	Present	Future	Imperfect	Preterite
yo	soy	seré	era	fui
tú	eres	serás	eras	fuiste
Él/ella/usted	es	será	era	fue
Nosotros/nosotras	somos	seremos	éramos	fuimos
Vosotros/vosotras	sois	seréis	erais	fuisteis
Ellos/ellas/ustedes	son	serán	eran	fueron

Usage of Ser

Ser is used to describe inherent characteristic or quality and conditions that are more or less permanent or long term.

Soy alto.I'm tall.

Él es pequeno.He is short.

Ella es divertida.She is funny.

El coche de Carlo es rojo.Carlo's car is red.

Mis hermanas son hermosas.My sisters are beautiful.

Arturo es un hombre inteligente.Arthur is an intelligent man.

Su familia es católica.Her family is Catholic.

Ser is used to express time, day, and hour:

¿Qué hora es?What time is it?

Es la una y diez.It's ten minutes after one o'clock.

Son las dos de la tarde. It's two o'clock in the afternoon.

Hoy es lunes.Today is Monday.

Es 5 de enero de 2017.It's January 5, 2017.

Ser is used to tell a person's origin or nationality.

¿De dónde eres?Where are you from?

Soy un americano.I'm an American.

Soy Estado Unidense.I'm from the United States.

Mi esposa es alemana.My wife is German.

Él es frances .He is French.

Ser is used to express relationships:

Carla es la esposa de Jaime.Carla is Jaime's wife.

Él es mi primo.He is my cousin.

Ser is used to tell a person's profession or occupation.

Soy contador.I'm an accountant.

Mis padres son abogados.My parents are lawyers.

Mi hermana es una maestra.My sister is a teacher.

Ser is used to indicate a person's marital status.

Soy soltero(a).I'm single.

Soy casado(a).I'm married.

Mi amigo es divorciado.My friend is divorced.

It is used to express possession:

Este libro es el mío.This book is mine.

Ese coche es el suyo.That car is his.

Ser is used with 'para' to express for whom something is intended:

El pastel es para mi sobrina.

The cake is for my niece.

Esta fiesta de cumpleaños es para mi madre.

This birthday party is for my mother.

Ser is used to tell the venue of an event:

El banquete es en el Grand Hotel.

The banquet is at the Grand Hotel.

Ser is used for impersonal expressions:

Es verdad. It's true.

Estar

Conjugation of the verb 'estar' in the four simple tenses:

Subject	Present	Future	Imperfect	Preterite
yo	estoy	estaré	estaba	estuve
tú	estás	estarás	estabas	estuviste
él/ella/usted	está	estará	estaba	estuvo
nosotros/nosotras	estamos	estaremos	estábamos	estuvimos
vosotros/vosotras	estáis	estaréis	estabais	estuvisteis
ellos/ellas/ustedes	están	estarán	estaban	estuvieron

Usage of estar

Estar is used to convey conditions which are temporary.

Estar is used to indicate or ask for physical or geographical locations:

¿Donde estan sus hijos?Where are your children?

Donna está en el mercado.Donna is in the market.

¿Dónde está Canadá?Where is Canada?

Estar is used with an adjective to express a changeable condition:

Carla está enferma.Carla is sick.

Estoy cansado(a).I'm tired.

¿Cómo está el pastel?How's the cake?

Su madre está enojada.His mother is angry.

¿Cómo estás?How are you?

Estoy bien.I'm well.

Estar is used to describe the weather, a constantly changing condition.

Está nevando.It's snowing.

Está nublado.It's cloudy.

Está lloviendo.It's raining.

Estar is used with a gerund to form progressive tenses.

In Spanish, a gerund is an invariable verb form which ends in –ndo for all verb groups. It is formed by dropping the infinitive endings and adding –ando (AR verbs) and –iendo (ER and IR verbs) to the stem.

Examples:

Estábamos durmiendo cuando llegó la tormenta.

We were sleeping when the storm arrived.

Estaba durmiendo cuando el perro mordió el niño.

I was sleeping when the dog bit the child.

Ser and Estar with Adjectives

Some adjectives convey an entirely different meaning depending on which verb they are used with.

Examples:

Ella está lista. (She is ready.)

Ella es lista. (She is clever.)

Carla está feliz. (Carla is happy).

Carla es feliz. (Carla is a happy person).

Él está vivo. (He is alive.)

Él es vivo. (He is lively.)

Ella está orgullosa. (She is proud.)

Ella es orgullosa. (She is conceited).

Él está callado. (He is quiet.)

Él es callado. (He is introverted.)

SIMPLE PAST TENSES

There are two past tenses in Spanish, the preterite and the imperfect.

Preterite

In general, the preterite is used to describe actions that were completed in the past. It indicates that the action has a definite beginning and that it happened within a specific time period.

Here are some phrases that indicate the use of the preterite:

ayeryesterday

anochelast night

el mes pasadolast month

la semana pasadalast week

entoncesthen

una vezone time

el año pasadolast year

el otro díathe other day

en ese momentoat that moment

To conjugate verbs in the preterite, you will drop the infinitive verb endings and add the following endings:

Subject	AR verbs	ER verbs	IR verbs
yo	-é	-í	-í
tú	-aste	-iste	-iste
él, ella, usted	-ó	-ió	-ió
nosotros, nosotras	-amos	-imos	-imos
vosotros, vosotras	-asteis	-isteis	-isteis
ellos, ellas, ustedes	-aron	-ieron	-ieron

Here is how you will conjugate the verbs hablar, comer, and escribir in the preterite:

Subject	**hablar**	**comer**	**escribir**
stem	**hab-**	**com-**	**escrib-**
yo	hablé	comí	escribí
tú	hablaste	comiste	escribiste
él/ella/usted	habló	comió	escribió

nosotros/nosotras	hablamos	comimos	escribimos
vosotros/vosotras	hablasteis	comisteis	escribisteis
ellos/ellas/ustedes	hablaron	comieron	escribieron

Examples:

Comimos el pastel ayer.

We ate cake yesterday.

Limpié mi cuarto la semana pasada.

I cleaned my room last week.

Le **escribí** una carta el mes pasado.

I wrote her a letter last month.

Bebieron el jugo de pomelo el martes pasado.

They drank pomelo juice last Tuesday.

The Imperfect Tense

The imperfect tense is used to denote past actions with no definite end. These may include actions that were habitually repeated in the past or to a general time in the past. It is used to describe a person's age, characteristics, or physical and mental condition in the past.

These expressions indicate the use of the imperfect tense:

cada díaevery day

cada semanaevery week

todos los díaseveryday

todos los añosevery year

cada mesevery month

cada añoevery year

a menudooften

a vecessometimes

rara vezrarely

frecuentementefrequently

siemprealways

generalmenteusually

muchas vecesmany times

algunas vecesat times

con frecuenciafrequently

mientraswhile

todas las semanasevery week

tantas vecesso many times

por lo generalgenerally

nuncanever

muchoa lot

casi nuncaalmost never

por un ratofor a while

varias vecesseveral times

todo el tiempoall the time

de vez en cuandoonce in a while

To conjugate verbs in the imperfect tense, you will have to add the following endings to the verb stem:

Subject	**AR verbs**	**ER verbs**	**IR verbs**
yo	-aba	-ía	-ía
tú	-abas	-ías	-ías
él/ella/usted	-aba	-ía	-ía
nosotros/nosotras	-ábamos	-íamos	-íamos
vosotros/vosotras	-abais	-íais	-íais
ellos/ellas/ustedes	-aban	-ían	-ían

To conjugate the verbs hablar, comer, and escribir in the imperfect:

Subject	hablar	comer	escribir
stem	hab-	com-	escrib-
yo	hablaba	comía	escribía
tú	hablabas	comías	escribías
él/ella/usted	hablaba	comía	escribía
nosotros/nosotras	hablábamos	comíamos	escribíamos
vosotros/vosotras	hablabais	comíais	escribíais
ellos/ellas/ustedes	hablaban	comían	escribían

Examples:

Limpiaba el cuarto cada dos días.

I used to clean the room every other day.

Vivía con mi tía por un rato.

I lived with my aunt for a while.

Ella **dormía** cuando llegamos.

She was sleeping when we arrived.

THE FUTURE TENSE

There are two ways to express the future tense in Spanish: the simple future and the informal future.

The Simple Future

To conjugate verbs in the simple future tense, you will retain the infinitive ending and simply add the prescribed personal ending. The three groups of verbs share the same ending in the simple future tense:

yo	-é
tú	-ás
él/ella/usted	-á
nosotros/nosotras	-emos
vosotros/vosotras	-éis
ellos/ellas/ustedes	-án

Hence, here is how you will conjugate the verbs hablar, beber, and abrir:

Subject	hablar	beber	abrir
yo	hablaré	beberé	abriré
tú	hablarás	beberás	abrirás
él/ella/usted	hablará	beberá	abrirá
nosotros/nosotras	hablaremos	beberemos	abriremos
vosotros/vosotras	hablaréis	beberéis	abriréis
ellos/ellas/ustedes	hablarán	beberán	abrirán

Uses of the Simple Future Tense

The Spanish simple future is most commonly used to express a guess or supposition:

Examples:

Probablemente visitaré a mi abuela el año próximo.

I will probably visit my grandmother next year.

Los niños tendrán hambre.

The children might be hungry.

The simple future is likewise used to make predictions or assumptions about the future but which outcome is uncertain or unknown.

For example:

Encontrará a un nuevo amigo.

He will find a new friend.

Mi hermano se casará con una mujer agradable.

My brother will marry a nice woman.

Take note that if you want to express something that is bound to happen or with reasonable certainty of happening in the future, you should use the present tense instead of the future tense.

Examples:

Se casa el 14 de febrero de 2017.

He is getting married on February 14, 2017.

Mis primos me visitan este sabado.

My cousins are going to visit me this Saturday.

Mis amigos vienen este sábado.

My friends are coming this Saturday.

Take note of several irregular verbs with different stems in the simple future:

InfinitiveStemMeaning

hacerhar-to make, to do

decirdir-to say

poderpodr-to be able

sabersabr-to know

haberhabr-to have

tenertendr-to have

ponerpondr-to put, place, set

quererquerr-to want, love

valervaldr-to be worth

venirvendr-to come

salirsaldr-to leave, go out

The Informal Future

The informal future is formed using the conjugated form of the verb 'ir' (to go) and the infinitive form of the verb:

present tense of ir + a + infinitive

The verb 'ir' takes the following forms in the present tense:

	ir (to go)
yo	voy
tú	vas
él/ella/usted	va
nosotros/nosotras	vamos
vosotros/vosotras	vais
ellos/ellas/ustedes	van

Examples:

Van a comprar en el centro comercial la semana próxima.

They will shop at the mall next week.

Él va a trabajar inmediatamente después del colegio.

He will work immediately after college.

Voy a comprar un vestido nuevo el próximo fin de semana.

I will buy a new dress next weekend.

The Perfect Tenses

The perfect tenses are compound tenses which are formed using an auxiliary verb and the past participle of the main verb.

Here are the perfect tenses in the indicative mood:

Present perfect

Past perfect

Future perfect

Perfect tenses express actions that are completed or perfected in the past, present, or future. It is formed with the conjugated form of haber and the past participle form of the main verb.

Past Participle

The past participle is formed by dropping the verb ending and adding the following ending:

AR verbs-ado

ER verbs-ido

IR verb-ido

Examples:

VerbPast participle

hablarhablado

comprarcomprado

comercomido

beberbebido

vivirvivido

salirsalido

Some verbs have irregular past participle forms. Here are the most commonly used ones:

abrirabierto

escribirescrito

hacerhecho

vervisto

decirdicho

volvervuelto

absolverabsuelto

satisfacersatisfecho

prenderpreso

ponerpuesto

romperroto

resolverresuelto

cubrircubierto

morirmuerto

freírfrito

The following verbs have irregular past participle form when used as an adjective but have regular forms when used as a verb:

Verb	Meaning	Adjective	Verb
despertar	to wake up	despierto	despertado
absorber	to absorb	absorto	absorbido
corrompe r	to corrupt	corrupto	corrumpido
poseer	to have	poseso	poseído
proveer	to provide	provisto	proveído
suspender	to hang	suspenso	suspendido
bendecir	to bless	bendito	bendecido
confundir	to confuse	confuso	confundido
imprimir	to print	impreso	imprimido
maldecir	to curse	maldito	maldecido
presumir	to presume	presunto	presumido

Haber

The verb haber is commonly used as an auxiliary verb in compound tenses. When used as such, it conveys the meaning 'to have'. This, however, does not imply possession and you must be careful not to confuse it with another irregular verb, tener (to have).

When used as an impersonal verb, haber takes the form 'hay' in the present indicative tense which is translated as 'there is' or 'there are'.

Examples:

Hay cinco libros en el escritorio.

There are five books on the desk.

Hay muchos niños en la playa.

There are many children on the beach.

When used as an auxiliary verb, haber has the following conjugations in the present indicative tense:

Subject	**haber**
yo	he
tú	has
él/ella/usted	ha
nosotros/nosotras	hemos
vosotros/vosotras	habéis
ellos/ellas/ustedes	han

The Present Perfect Tense

The present perfect tense is used to denote a condition or an action that has been completed or has occurred prior to the present time. The present indicative form of haber is used with the past participle form of the verb to form the present perfect tense.

Examples:

He hablado.

I have spoken.

Hemos decidido asistir a la fiesta.

We have decided to attend the party.

Ha escrito una carta a su amigo.

He has written a letter to his friend.

Has terminado las especulaciones.

You have ended the speculations.

Han dimitido de su trabajo.

They have resigned from their job.

The Past Perfect Tense

The past perfect tense conveys an action that was completed at some point in the past before another event or action has occurred. The imperfect form of haber is paired with the past participle to form the past perfect tense.

Imperfect forms of haber:

Subject	haber
yo	había
tú	habías
él/ella/usted	había
nosotros/nosotras	habíamos

vosotros/vosotras	habíais
ellos/ellas/ustedes	habían

Examples:

El sospechoso **había limpiado** la habitación antes de que los policías llegaron.

The suspect had cleaned the room before the policemen arrived.

(Ellos) **habían hablado** contra la minería irresponsable.

They had spoken against irresponsible mining.

Había caminado tres millas al mediodía.

I had walked three miles by noon.

The Future Perfect Tense

The future perfect tense expresses an action that will have been completed at some point in the future. To form the future perfect tense, you'll use the future form of haber and the past participle.

Future forms of haber

Subject	haber
yo	habré
tú	habrás
él/ella/usted	habrá
nosotros/nosotras	habremos
vosotros/vosotras	habréis
ellos/ellas/ustedes	Habrán

Examples:

Habré ahorrado veinte mil dólares antes del próximo año.

I will have saved twenty thousand dollars by next year.

Habrá entrado en el concurso de matemáticas por el mes que viene.

She will have entered the mathematics competition by next month.

REFLEXIVE VERBS

Reflexive verbs denote an action that a person is performing towards himself or herself. A verb is reflexive if its subject and direct object are one. Reflexive verbs are frequently used in Spanish and they typically convey actions or activities related to personal routines such as taking a bath, combing one's hair, or brushing one's teeth. A reflexive verb requires a reflexive pronoun as a receiver of the action.

The infinitive form of a reflexive verb ends in –se which can translate to 'oneself'.

Examples

vestirseto dress oneself

cepillarseto brush oneself

lavarseto wash oneself

To conjugate a reflexive verb, drop the –se ending and conjugate normally. The reflexive pronoun which acts as the receiver of the action is placed before the verb. Reflexive pronouns must agree with the subject in both gender and number.

Here are the reflexive pronouns and the subject pronouns they refer to:

Subject Pronouns	Reflexive Pronouns
yo	me
tú	te
él/ella/usted	se
nosotros/nosotras	nos
vosotros/vosotras	os
ellos/ellas/ustedes	se

Examples:

(Yo) me baño.

I bathe (myself).

(Ella) se viste para el banquete.

She dresses herself for the party.

(Ellos) se despertaron temprano.

They woke up early.

Placement of Reflexive Pronouns

Reflexive pronouns are placed before the verb. They may also be found at the end of the verb. Whenever the infinitive form is used, you must add the pronoun at the end of the verb.

Examples:

Quiero ducharme.

I want to bathe myself.

Debo afeitarme.

I have to shave myself.

The reflexive construction is likewise used to indicate ownership. In English, you will usually do this with a possessive adjective. In Spanish, since the reflexive construction clearly shows that the object is owned by the subject, you can use a definite article before the body part or the object.

For example:

Me lavo las manos. I wash my hands.

Most commonly used reflexive verbs:

bañarse	to bathe
alegrarse (de)	to be glad about
disgustarse (de)	to be upset about
convertirse (en)	to become
volverse	to become
enfermarse	to become ill
cepillarse	to brush
peinarse	to comb one's hair
taparse	to cover up oneself
distraerse	to distract oneself
secarse	to dry off
desayunarse	to eat breakfast
divertirse (con)	to enjoy oneself with
limarse (las uñas)	to file
olvidarse (de)	to forget about
reponerse	to get better
aburrirse (de)	to get bored with
vestirse	to get dressed
enojarse (con)	to get mad about
arreglarse	to get onself ready
desvestirse	to get undressed

subirse	to get up
levantarse	to get up
enloquecerse	to go crazy
acostarse	to go to bed
dormirse	to go to sleep
irse	to leave
mirarse	to look at oneself
ponerse	to put on
pintarse (los labios)	to put on lipstick
maquillarse	to put on makeup
acordarse (de)	to remember
despedirse	to say good-bye
afeitarse	to shave
afeitarse	to shave oneself
ducharse	to shower
sentarse	to sit down
sostenerse	to support
quitarse	to take off
probarse	to try on
torcerse	to twist
destaparse	to uncover
despertarse	to wake up

CHAPTER 7: ADJECTIVES

Before continue, please refer to your audiobook companion PDF that comes free with your purchase of this audiobook in order to see all the illustrative tables inside while learning Spanish language.

Adjectives are words that modify a noun or a pronoun. In Spanish, adjectives must agree in number and gender with the words they describe. Hence, an adjective can have four forms.

For example:

el libro nuevolos libros nuevos

la casa nuevalas casas nuevas

An adjective will normally appear in a dictionary in its singular masculine form. Hence, you must know how to form the feminine and the plural form.

Most singular adjectives end in –o but there are also many adjectives that end in –e, -ista, or a consonant. Here are quick guidelines that will help you form the feminine and the plural for adjectives:

Adjectives ending in –o

Adjectives that end in –o have four forms to match the gender and number of the word they describe. They form the plural by adding –s at the end of the word. Here are the endings for this group of adjectives:

MasculineFeminine

Singular -o -a

Plural -os -as

Examples:

el hombre alto (the tall man)los hombres altos (the tall men)

la mujer alta (the tall woman)las mujeres altas (the tall women)

Adjectives ending in –e or ista

Adjectives that end in –e or –ista have similar forms for the masculine and feminine gender but have two forms to describe the singular and plural nouns.

Adjectives ending in –e:

Singular-e

Plural-es

The above endings indicate that you will only need to add –s to the adjective in its singular form.

Examples:

Mi padre es amable.My father is friendly.

Mi madre es amable.My mother is friendly.

Mis padres son amables.My parents are friendly.

Adjectives with –ista ending:

Adjectives ending in –ista have the following endings in the singular and plural:

Singular-ista

Plural-istas

This means that to form their plural, you will have to add –s to their ending in the singular form.

Examples:

Mi hermano es optimista.My brother is optimistic.

Mi hermana es optimista.My sister is optimistic.

Mis hermanos son optimistas.My brothers are optimistic.

Mis hermanas son optimistas.My sisters are optimistic.

Adjectives ending in a consonant

Most adjectives that end in a consonant have similar forms for masculine and feminine but change their form to agree with the number of the word they describe.

To form their plural, you will add –es to the singular form.

Examples:

El examen es difícil.The examination is difficult.

Los exámenes son difíciles.The examinations are difficult.

However, take note of the following exceptions:

Adjectives ending in –z in the singular change their ending from z to c before adding –es.

Example:

El perro es feroz.Los perros son feroces.

Adjectives ending in –or, –ón, -an, and -ín

Adjectives that end in –or, –ón, -an, and -ín have feminine forms. To form the feminine, simply add –a (singular) or –as (plural) to the masculine singular form and drop the written accent when needed.

Examples:

Mi amigo es hablador.

Mi amiga es habladora.

My friend is talkative.

Mis amigos son habladores.

My friends are talkative.

Mis amigas son habladoras.

My friends are talkative.

PLACEMENT OF ADJECTIVES

In English, adjectives are always placed before the word they modify. In Spanish, however, adjectives generally come after the noun they modify.

Examples:

el niño juguetónthe playful boy

la niña rubia blonde girl

el atleta valientethe brave athlete

la chica simpaticathe nice girl

Some adjectives can come before the noun they modify.

Adjectives may be placed before the noun to emphasize its inherent quality:

el valiente leónel azul cielo

the brave lionthe blue sky

la dulce miella blanca nieve

the sweet honeythe white snow

las verdes hojasla bella flor

the green leavesthe beautiful flower

An adjective may also appear before the noun to emphasize its special quality.

For instance, to stress that Maria is such a good singer:

Maria es una buena cantante.

Limiting adjectives are placed before the noun they modify.

Limiting adjectives are words that restrict the amount, quality, or quantity of a noun. This group of adjectives includes numbers, possessive adjectives, moral qualifiers not otherwise introduced by adverbial modifiers, comparative and superlative adjectives mejor (best) and peor (worst), as well as some words that indicate quantity.

Here are examples of quantity words that function as limiting adjectives:

algunosome

todoall

pocoa little

ningunono, none

suficienteenough, sufficient

cuantoas much

mucho many

menosless

variossome, few

bastanteenough

Examples:

Maria necesita algunos trabajadores.

Maria needs some workers.

Él tiene muchos amigos.

He has many friends.

Tengo tres hermanos y una hermana.

I have three brothers and one sister.

Hoy es el mejor día de mi vida.

Today is the best day of my life.

Some adjectives convey a different meaning according to their placement. Here are some examples:

Adjective	Adjective Placement	
	Before the noun	After the noun
alto	top, high-class	tall
bueno	simple, good	good, gentle, generous
cierto	certain	true, right
dulce	good, nice	sweet
grande	great	big
medio	average	half
mismo	same	himself/herself, very
nuevo	different, another	new
pobre	poor: unfortunate	poor: penniless
propio	his, her own	proper
raro	rare	strange
simple	mere	simple
triste	dreadful	sad
único	only	unique
varios	several	different
viejo	former	old, aged

Shortened Adjective Forms

Some adjectives take shortened forms when placed before a masculine singular noun. These adjectives drop the final –o but retain the original meaning in the short forms. This process is called apocopation and the shortened form is called an apócope.

Examples:

buenobuenel buen rey (the good king)

malomalmal cocinero (bad cook)

primeroprimerel primer amor (first love)

tercerotercerel tercer edificio (third building)

unounun hombre (a man)

algunoalgúnalgún día (some day)

ningunoningúnningún regalo (no gift)

The word 'Santo' takes the shortened form 'San' when placed before a singular masculine noun except when the noun starts with 'Do' or 'To'.

San PedroSaint Peter

San PabloSaint Paul

San FranciscoSaint Francis

Santo DomingoSaint Dominic

Santo TomásSaint Thomas

Some adjectives have shortened forms regardless of the gender of the noun that comes after them:

cientocien niñas (one hundred girls)

cualquieracualquier mujer (any woman)

grandeun gran edificio (a great building)

Multiple Adjectives

In Spanish, you can use a series of adjectives to describe a noun. They can be placed before or after the noun or scattered in different parts.

To emphasize the noun's characteristics or inherent qualities, you can place one or more adjectives before the noun:

Mi padre es un inteligente y valiente caballero.

My father is an intelligent and brave gentleman.

You can place two or more adjectives after a noun to restrict or clarify the noun:

Él es un hombre intelligente y valiente.

He is an intelligent and brave man.

You can split multiple adjectives by placing the subjective ones before the noun and the objectives one after it.

Él es un gran cantante canadiense.
He is a great Canadian singer.

Most Commonly Used Adjectives

Spanish	English
agresivo	aggressive
enojado	angry
enfadoso	annoying
malo	bad
bello	beautiful
hermoso	beautiful
querido	beloved
mejor	better
grande	big
amargo	bitter
ciego	blind
hervido	boiled
aburrido	bored
quebrado	broken
quemado	burnt
tranquilo	calm
capaz	capable
cuidadoso	careful
caritativo	charitable
barato	cheap
limpio	clean
claro	clear
frío	cold
confortable	comfortable
complicado	complicated
contento	satisfied
fresco	cool
correcto	correct
cortés	courteous
loco	insane

cruel	cruel
curioso	curious, odd
oscuro	dark
sordo	deaf
delicioso	delicious
sabroso	delicious
difícil	difficult
duro	difficult
aplicado	diligent
sucio	dirty
descortés	discourteous
borracho	drunk
seco	dry
temprano	early
fácil	easy
comestible	edible
vacío	empty
divertido	entertaining
igual	equal
excelente	excellent
caro	expensive, dear
apagable	extinguishable
rápido	fast
gordo	fat
favorito	favorite
feroz	ferocious
cochino	filthy, nasty
llano	flat, even
extraño	foreign, strange
rompible	fragile, breakable
oloroso	fragrant
libre	free
frito	fried
amable	friendly

helado	frozen
lleno	full
cómico	funny
apacible	gentle
bueno	good
grave	grave
culpable	guilty
guapo	handsome
alegre	happy
feliz	happy
sano	healthy
pesado	heavy
honesto	honest
caliente	hot
húmedo	humid
ignorante	ignorant
analfabeto	illiterate
inteligente	intelligent
interesante	interesting
corajudo	irritable
celoso	jealous
tarde	late
flojo	lazy, loose
perezoso	lazy
poco	little, few
largo	long
perdido	lost
cariñoso	loving
hecho	made
magnífico	magnificent
mucho	many, much
casado	married
maduro	mature, ripe
travieso	mischievous

modesto	modest
baboso	moronic
móvil	moveable
mudo	mute
desnudo	naked
encuerado	naked
estrecho	narrow
natural	natural
nervioso	nervous
nuevo	new
ruidoso	noisy
antiguo	old
viejo	old
doloroso	painful
pálido	pale
paciente	patient
simpático	pleasant
venenoso	poisonous
pobre	poor
embarazada	pregnant
bonito	pretty
profundo	profound
orgulloso	proud
listo	ready, quick-witted
rico	rich
asado	roasted
pudrido	rotten
redondo	round-shaped
corriente	running, flowing
triste	sad
salado	salty
asustado	scared

severo	severe, harsh
corto	short
vergonzoso	shy
enfermo	sick
sencillo	simple
flaco	skinny, thin
despacio	slow
lento	slow
pequeño	small
apestoso	smelly
picante	spicy, sharp
fuerte	strong
tonto	stupid
superior	superior, better
sospechoso	suspicious
dulce	sweet
alto	tall, high
doméstico	tame
grueso	thick
delgado	thin
cansado	tired
feo	ugly
inolvidable	unforgettable
único	unique, sole
usado	used
inútil	useless
tibio	warm, tepid
débil	weak
mojado	wet
ancho	wide
salvaje	wild, savage
sabio	wise
joven	young

DEMONSTRATIVE ADJECTIVES

Demonstrative adjectives describe the noun they refer to in terms of its distance from the speaker. There are three types of demonstrative adjectives and each of them has four forms to agree with the number and gender of the noun they modify.

Demonstrative adjectives that describe nouns which are close to the speaker's location (this/these):

	Singular	Plural
Masculine	este (this)	estos (these)
Feminine	esta (this)	estas (these)

Este libro es mío. This book is mine.

Esta casa es pequeña. This house is small.

Estos libros son interesantes. These books are interesting.

Estas faldas son bonitas. These skirts are pretty.

Demonstrative adjectives that describe a noun which is not close to the speaker (that/those):

	Singular	Plural
Masculine	ese (that)	esos (those)
Feminine	esa (that)	esas (those)

Esa gata es divertida. That cat is funny.

Quiero esa falda azul. I want that blue skirt.

Esos pendientes son costosos. Those earrings are expensive.

Esas muñecas son bonitas. Those dolls are pretty.

Demonstrative adjectives that describe noun or nouns which are far from the speaker (that/those over there):

	Masculine	Feminine
Singular	aquel (that over there)	aquella (that over there)
Plural	aquellos (those over there)	aquellas (those over there)

Aquel hombre es un buen cantante.

That man is a good singer.

Aquella cobra es peligrosa.

That cobra is dangerous.

Me gustan aquellas flores.

I like those flowers.

Aquellas sillas son de madera de roble.

Those chairs are made of oakwood.

Demonstrative Adjective Placement

Demonstrative adjectives are generally placed before the noun they modify. If more than one noun is being described, each should be modified by an appropriate demonstrative adjective.

Examples:

Esa casa y este coche son caros.

That house and this car are expensive.

Aquellas camisas y esos pantalones son bonitos.

Those shirts and those pants are pretty.

CHAPTER 8: PREPOSITIONS, ADVERBS, AND CONJUNCTIONS

PREPOSITIONS

A preposition connects words together and establishes a relationship between them. In general, prepositions are invariable words. Except when the prepositions 'a' and 'de' contract with the definite article 'el' to form 'al' and 'del', prepositions do not vary with gender or number. They are usually placed before a noun, a pronoun, or a verb used as a noun.

Los visitantes son de España.The visitors are from Spain.

Los niños van al zoológico.The children are going to the zoo.

Este pastel es para mi madre.This cake is for my mother.

Caminamos en el parque.We strolled in the park.

Corrió hacia su madre.He ran towards his mother.

Prepositions

a	to, for, by, at
al	upon
al lado de	beside
ante	before
antes de	before
bajo	under
cerca de	near
como	like
con	with
contra	against
de	of, from, about
debajo de	beneath, under
debido a	due to
delante de	in front of
dentro de	inside
dentro de	inside, within
desde	since

después de	after
detrás de	behind
durante	during
en vez de	instead of
en	in, on, at, about
en	in, on, at, about
encima de	on top, above
enfrente de	in front of
entre	among, between
fuera de	outside
hacia	towards
hasta	until
incluso	including
lejos de	far from
menos	except
para	for
por	on account of, for
salvo	except
según	according to
sin	without
sobre	on, above, about
tras	after
vía	via

ADVERBS

Adverbs are words that provide more details to sentences by describing verbs, adjectives, and other adverbs. They are invariable words that provide more information on manner, time, quantity, intensity, and frequency.

Forming adverbs

Adverbs are usually formed by adding the suffix –mente to the feminine singular form of adjectives. This is similar to the suffix –ly in English.

For instance, to express 'Marina talks slowly', you can add –mente to lenta, the feminine singular form of the adjective lento (slow), to form lentamente. Hence:

Marina habla lentamente.

Here are other examples of adverbs of manner:

Masculine	Feminine	Adverb	Meaning
alegre	alegre	alegremente	happily
breve	breve	brevemente	briefly
claro	clara	claramente	clearly
cortés	cortés	cortésmente	courteously
especial	especial	especialmente	specially
fácil	fácil	fácilmente	easily
final	final	finalmente	finally
frecuente	frecuente	frecuentemente	frequently
paciente	paciente	pacientemente	patiently
rápido	rápida	rápidamente	quickly
sincero	sincera	sinceramente	sincerely

Examples:

Esperó pacientemente a su amiga.

She waited patiently for her friend.

Habló claramente en la fiesta.

He spoke clearly at the party.

Agradeció sinceramente a su madre.

He sincerely thanked his mother.

Forming adverbial phrases with 'con'

You can form adverbial phrases by using the preposition 'con' (with) with a noun.

Examples:

Adverbial PhraseMeaning

con claridadclearly

con cortesíacourteously

con alegríahappily

con rapidezrapidly

con perfecciónperfectly

con respetorespectfully

con habilidadskillfully

Besides adverbs of manner which are formed with –mente and –con, there are several adverbs in Spanish that will help you convey information on manner, time, place, quantity, frequency, affirmation, and negation:

Adverbs of Manner	
alderedor	around
bajo	softly
alto	loudly
mejor	better
peor	worse
duro	hard
bien	well
muy	very
sereno	calmly
mal	badly or poorly
así	so, like this

Mi hermana es **muy** hermosa.

My sister is very beautiful.

Trabajó **duro** para su familia.

He worked hard for his family.

Adverbs of Time	
aún	yet, still

ayer	yesterday
después	later, after
ahora	now
ya	already
hoy	today
anoche	last night
luego	soon
temprano	early
mientras	while
tarde	late
entonces	then
a veces	sometimes
pronto	soon
todavía	yet, still
todavía no	not yet
mañana	tomorrow
cuando	when

Ella llegó **temprano**.She arrived early.

Fue a la escuela **hoy**.She went to the school today.

Adverbs of Place	
adelante	in front/ahead
abajo	downstairs
arriba	upstairs, above
por arriba	up there
detrás	behind
enfrente	in front of
por delante	in front
dentro	inside
adentro	inside
por abajo	down there
todas	everywhere

partes	
lejos	far
aquí	here
por atrás	in back
donde	where
debajo	under
ahi	there
allí	over there
cerca	nearby
del lugar	of place
encima	on top, above
acá	over here
afuera	outside
fuera	outside
alguna parte	somewhere
allá	over there
por acá	around here
paraallá	that way
paraacá	this way

Se esconde **dentro**.

He is hiding inside.

Estoy parado **aquí**.

I'm standing here.

Los gatitos están jugando **debajo** de la cama.

The kittens are playing under the bed.

Adverbs of Quantity	
mucho	a lot
poco	little, few
bastante	enough
más	more
menos	less

demasiado	too much
casi	almost
suficiente	enough
apenas	hardly
tanto	so much, as much

La comida es **apenas** suficiente para ellos.

The food is hardly enough for them.

Están **casi** terminados.

They are almost finished.

Adverbs of Frequency	
siempre	always
a veces	sometimes
frecuentemente	frequently
raramente	rarely
rara vez	rarely
semanalmente	weekly
anualmente	yearly
cada hora	every hour
casi nunca	seldom
nunca	never

Mi madre está **siempre** en casa.

My mother is always at the house.

Raramente comemos la carne.

We rarely eat meat.

Other Adverbs:

Adverbs of Affirmation	
si	yes
ciertamente	for sure

verdaderamente	for sure
tambien	also
seguramente	surely
efectivamente	for sure
asimismo	as well
en efecto	in fact
cierto	that's right
desde luego	of course

Adverbs of Negation	
nunca	never
jamás	never
nada	nothing
tampoco	neither
ni	nor
no	no
ni…no	neither…nor

Interrogative Adverbs	
¿adónde?	Where to?
¿cómo?	How?
¿cuándo?	When?
¿cuánto?	How many/much?
¿dónde?	Where?
¿por que?	Why?

Adverbs of Opinion	
quizás	perhaps
evidentemente	obviously
personalmente	personally

CONJUNCTIONS

A conjunction is a word that joins words, phrases, or clauses together. There are three types of conjunctions in Spanish: coordinating, subordinating, and correlative conjunctions.

Coordinating Conjuctions

A coordinating conjunction connects words or clauses of similar kind or function.

y	and
o	or
pero	but
pues	then
entonces	thus, so
sino	but

Take note that when the conjunction 'y' is placed before a word that starts with 'i' or 'hi', 'y' changes to 'e' to avoid pronouncing successive 'i' sound and thus ease pronunciation.

Similarly, the conjunction 'o' changes to 'u' when used before a word that starts with 'o' or 'ho'.

In addition, 'o' changes to 'ó' when placed between numbers. Hence: to express 'six or seven', you will write: 5 ó 3.

Examples:

Juego el tenis y leo libros cada fin de semana.

I play tennis and read books every weekend.

Habla francés, alemán, español e inglés.

He speaks French, German, Spanish, and English.

Ama su marido pero no puede olvidar su infidelidad.

She loves her husband but she cannot forget his infidelity.

Subordinating Conjuctions

Subordinating conjunctions connect a dependent (subordinate) clause to an independent (main) clause.

Here are the commonly used subordinating conjunctions:

tan pronto como	as soon as
como	as, since
porque	because
antes (de) que	before

aunque	even though
asi que	therefore
bien que	even though
como quiera que	since, although
pues	for, because
si	if
así	just as
además	also
en caso de que	in case
mientras que	while, whereas
siempre que	provided that
empero	yet
puesto que	since
ya que	since
a fin de que	so that
para que	so that
que	that
a menos que	unless
hasta que	until
cuando	when
sin que	without
a pesar de que	in spite of

Examples:

No puede jugar el fútbol **porque** está enfermo.

He can't play football because he's sick.

Miraré la película **si** no estoy ocupado este fin de semana.

I will watch the movie if I'm not busy this weekend.

El perro ladró fuertemente **cuando** el cartero llamó.

The dog barked loudly when the postman called.

Correlative Conjunctions

Correlative conjunctions show the relation between different ideas in a sentence and are always used in pairs.

The following are examples of correlative conjunctions:

o…o	either…or
ni…ni	neither…nor
sea…sea	either…or
bien…bien	either…or
uno…otro	one…another
tal…tal	this…that
ora…ora	now…now
cual…cual	like…like
ya…ya	whether…or
que…que	or

Examples:

Ni Rica **ni** Selina fue elegido como candidato para el desfile.

Neither Rica nor Selina was chosen as candadiate for the pageant.

Él es **o** un criminal **o** un héroe.

He is either a criminal or a hero.

Chapter 9: Forming Sentences

Sentence Patterns

To form a basic sentence, you need a subject and a verb. To these two elements, you can add other elements such as direct objects, indirect objects, or prepositional phrases. The basic pattern is identical to the subject-verb-object (S-V-O) pattern in English.

For example:

Yo leo libros.I read books.

S V O

Él come el pastel.He eats cake.

S V O

Native speakers typically drop the subject as the conjugated verb clearly shows who or what is the subject. Hence, the following are complete sentences:

Leo libros.I read books.

Come pastel.He eats cake.

Spanish word order is more flexible than English word order. You can rearrange words in a sentence to highlight a different grammatical element without changing the idea.

For example:

Yo leo libros. The sentence indicates that it is me who reads the books and not another person.

Libros leo.The sentence emphasizes that I read books instead of magazines or other reading materials.

Leo libros.The sentence emphasizes the act of reading the books instead of giving them away or storing them.

DECLARATIVE SENTENCES

In general, declarative sentences use this pattern:

subject + predicate + object

Example:

Janna vende coches.Janna sells cars.

Michelle hornea un pastel.Michelle bakes a cake.

When an object pronoun takes the place of the noun object, the object pronoun is placed before the verb.

Janna los vende.Janna sells them (cars).

Myra lo hornea.Myra bakes it (the cake).

When a sentence has a direct and indirect object, the direct object is usually placed before the indirect object.

Example:

Janna vende coches a sus amigas.

Janna sells cars to her friends.

Myra hornea un pastel para su madre.

Myra bakes a cake for her mother.

Adverbs are generally placed near the word they modify. When they modify adjective and averbs, they are usually placed before the word they modify. When they modify verbs, they are usually found after the verb.

Examples:

Mi amiga es muy agradable.

My friend is very nice.

Vin juega el tenis frecuentemente.

Vin plays tennis frequently.

Spanish sentence pattern is quite flexible and you will most probably see the above statements in a different word order such as the following:

Frecuentemente, Vin juega el tenis.

Frequently, Vin plays tennis.

Vin frecuentemente juega el tenis.

Vin frequently plays tennis.

INTERROGATIVE SENTENCES

Interrogative sentences generally begin with an inverted question mark and a regular question mark at the end. There are several ways of forming yes-no questions in Spanish.

To form a declarative sentence, simply switch the subject and the verb.

For example:

Declarative sentence:Marina cose.Marina sews.

Interrogative sentence:¿Cose Marina?Does Marina sew?

Another way to ask a question is by simply raising the tone when asking verbally.

For example, read the following and raise your tone at the end of the sentence:

¿Martha cocina?Martha cooks?

In English, you can form questions by adding tag words such as 'is it?', 'right', 'isn't it?' at the end of the sentence. You can also form questions in Spanish by adding tag words.

Examples:

Marina cose, ¿no?

Martha cocina, ¿es verdad?

Take note that the inverted question mark was only placed at the start of the tag question words.

Negative Sentences

To form negative sentences, simply place the word 'no' before the verb.

For example:

Él toca la guitarra.Él no toca la guitarra.

He plays the guitar.He doesn't play the guitar.

Yo escribo canciones.Yo no escribo canciones.

I write songs.I don't write songs.

CHAPTER 10: THE SUBJUNCTIVE & IMPERATIVE MOOD

THE SUBJUNCTIVE MOOD

The subjunctive mood is used to convey doubts, wishes, emotions, hypothetical situations, and uncertainties. It is used to express opinion, make recommendations, or express feelings. While the indicative mood is an objective mood, the subjunctive mood is generally subjective. The subjunctive mood is commonly used in Spanish and it includes almost all tenses found in the indicative mood.

A sentence in the subjunctive mood generally has three parts:

Two subjects

A subjunctive sentence will have one subject each in the main clause and the subordinate clause.

Two verbs

The main clause has one verb in the indicative mood which will trigger the subjunctive mood. The subordinate clause has a separate verb in the subjunctive mood.

Relative pronoun (que, quien, como)

The relative pronoun is the link between the main clause and the subordinate clause.

Here are examples of sentences in the subjunctive mood:

Es posible que Marty hable francés.

It's possible that Marty speaks French.

Es probable que llegue tarde a la fiesta.

It's likely that he will arrive late at the party.

Take note of the following phrases which generally indicate the use of the subjunctive mood:

It is good that ___Es bueno que ___

It's better that __Más vale que ___

It is bad that __Es malo que ___

It is doubtful that__Es dudoso que___

It is not certain that ___No es cierto que ___

It's preferable that__Es preferible que___

It is not likely that ___Es difícil que ___

Conjugating the Verb in the Present Subjunctive Mood

To conjugate verbs in the present subjunctive mood, you will use the first person singular form of the verb and drop the –o ending. Following are the personal endings for the present tense in the subjunctive mood:

AR Verbs:

yo	-e
tú	-es
él/ella/usted	-e
nosotros/nosotras	-emos
vosotros/vosotras	-éis
ellos/ellas/ustedes	-en

ER and IR Verbs

yo	-a
tú	-as
él/ella/usted	-a
nosotros/nosotras	-amos
vosotros/vosotras	-áis
ellos/ellas/ustedes	-an

THE IMPERATIVE MOOD

The imperative mood is used for stating a direct command or for telling someone to do something. Since there are two ways of addressing a person in Spanish, the formal and the informal, commands can take different forms.

Informal (tú) commands

The affirmative tú command is used when you're addressing a command to a family member, a friend, a pet, or someone you would normally address informally. The negative tú command is used to tell the same group not to do something.

Affirmative Informal or tú Commands

To express a familiar command, you will use the present indicative third person singular form.

	-ar verbs	-er verbs	-ir verbs
tú	-a	-e	-e

Hence, the verbs comprar (to buy), comer (to eat), and abrir (to open) will have the following forms in the imperative:

	comprar	comer	abrir
tú	compra	come	abre

Examples:

Compra el bolso.Buy the bag.

¡Come las verduras!Eat the vegetables!

¡Abre la puerta!Open the door!

Spelling changes for stem-changing verbs in the present tense are maintained when these verbs are used in the imperative.

Examples:

Encontrar (to find)¡Encuentra el libro!Find the book!

Mover (to move)¡Mueve la silla!Move the chair!

Dormir (to sleep)¡Duerme ahora!Sleep now!

Irregular Affirmative Informal Commands

Some verbs have irregular forms in the imperative mood.

Examples:

ser (to be)sé

hacer (to make)haz

tener (to have)ten

decir (to tell)di

ir (to go)ve

salir (to leave)sal

poner (to put)pon

venir (to come, arrive)ven

¡Ve ahora!Go now!

¡Di la verdad!Tell the truth!

¡Sal ahora!Leave now!

Pronoun Placement

A pronoun used in an affirmative command is attached to the end of the verb. In addition, an accent mark is added to the verb to retain its original stress.

Examples:

¡Díselo! Tell it to her!

¡Cómpramelo!Buy it for me.

¡Tráeselo!Bring it to him.

Punctuations in Imperative Sentences

The use of exclamation points or naming the receiver of the command clarifies the subject of the verb and helps avoid confusion with the present indicative third person singular form when writing imperative sentences.

Compare these sentences:

Present indicative

Compra el bolso.He buys the bag.

Informal command

¡Compra el bolso!Buy the bag!

Present indicative

Annie compra el bolso.Annie buys the bag.

Informal command

Annie, ¡compra el bolso¡Annie, buy the bag!

Negative Informal or tú Commands

A negative informal command is formed by placing no before the tú form in the present subjunctive.

Present subjuctive tú forms:

AR verbs	-es
ER verbs	-as
IR verbs	-as

Hence, the verbs comprar, comer, and abrir will have the following forms in the negative:

	comprar	comer	abrir
tú	compres	comas	abras

Examples:

No compres el bolso.Don't buy the bag.

¡No comas el pastel!Don't eat the cake!

¡No abras la caja!Don't open the box!

Formal commands – Affirmative and Negative

The formal command is used to address people who are older, new acquaintances, and people you would normally address formally like a superior, teacher, government officials, or a religious leader. Except for Spain, Spanish-speaking countries only use the formal command to address all people.

Whether you're using an affirmative or negative command, the formal command uses the present subjunctive form of the verb.

	AR verbs	ER verbs	IR verbs
usted	-e	-a	-a
ustedes	-en	-an	-an

Affirmative formal commands

Examples:

comprar (to buy)Compre el bolso para mi, por favor.

Please buy the bag for me.

ser (to be)Sea amable a la personas mayores.

Be polite to older people.

abrir (to open)Abra la puerta.

Please open the door.

Ustedes:

pagar (to pay)Paguen la cuenta, por favor.

Please pay the bill.

comer (to eat)Señoras coman por favor.

Mesdames, please eat.

abrir (to open)Abran sus bolsas.

Please open your bags.

Negative Formal Commands

To form the negative formal command, add a negative word before the affirmative formal command.

Examples:

No hablen por favor.Please don't speak.

No abran sus bolsas.Don't open your bags.

No paguen la cuenta.Don't pay the bill.

No coman, por favor.Don't eat, please.

Pronoun placement in Affirmative commands

Object pronouns are attached immediately at the end of the verb in the imperative mood. When both direct and indirect object pronouns are used, the indirect object pronoun is placed before the direct object pronoun. When verbs have more than one syllable, a written accent is used to maintain its original stress.

Buy it.Cómprelo Ud.

Eat it.Cómalo.

Bring it to me.Tráigamelo.

Pronoun Placement in Negative Commands

In formal negative commands, the object pronoun appears before the verb and after the negative word.

Don't buy it for them.No se los compre.

CHAPTER 11: MAKING COMPARISONS

There are different ways to make comparisons in Spanish. You can compare adjectives, verbs, or adverbs. You can make comparisons of equality or inequality and absolute or relative superlative.

COMPARISONS OF EQUALITY

The comparison of equality is used to compare things of equal qualities or characteristics.

You will use the following format for this type of comparison:

To compare with adjectives or adverbs

tan + adjective/adverb + como

When using an adjective to make comparisons, it should agree with the number and gender of the first noun.

Ella es tan bella como su madre.

She is as beautiful as her mother.

Mi padre es tan bueno como mi madre.

My father is as good as my mother.

To compare with nouns

tanto/tanta/tantos/tantas + noun + como

Tanto should agree with the noun in gender and number. Hence:

Marco tiene tantas amigas como Francisco.

Marco has as many female friends as Francisco.

Ella tiene tantas bolsas como su amiga.

She has as many bags as her friend.

To compare with verbs:

verb + tanto + como

Karen trabaja tanto como Ricardo.

Karen works as much as Ricardo.

COMPARISONS OF INEQUALITY

Comparion of inequality refers to the comparison of two unequal objects or people in which one has more or less of a particular characteristic or quality.

Here is the format for comparing adjectives or adverbs:

más/menos + adjective/adverb + que

Carlota es más alta que Marita.

Carlota is taller than Marita.

Soy menos inteligente que mi hermano.

I am less intelligent than my brother.

Verbs can also be used to make comparisons:

Usted estudia más que su amiga.

You study more than your friend does.

Comparisons with Superlatives

Relative Superlative

Relative superlative expresses that one or more people or object has the greatest or the least degree of a specific quality relative to others in the group.

You will use this pattern for this type of comparison:

subject + verb + el/la/los/las + más/menos + adjective + de + group

Marian es la más activa de la clase.

Marian is the most active of the class.

Es la menos costosa de las opciones.

It's the least expensive of all the options.

Absolute Superlative

Absolute superlative expresses a greater degree of characteristic or quality. It is formed by adding –érrimo(a), –bilísimo(a), or ísimo(a).

Examples:

amable (kind)amabilísima (extremely kind)

celebre (famous)celebérrimo (extremely famous)

bella (beautiful)bellísima (extremely beautiful)

Irregular Comparison

Irregular comparison involves the use of irregular comparison words similar to the words 'bad' or 'worse' in English.

The following are the irregular comparison words in Spanish:

Adjectives

PositiveComparative

joven (young)menor (younger)

viejo (old)mayor (older)

pequeño (little)menor (littler/younger)

grande (big)mayor (bigger/older)

bueno (good)mejor (better)

malo (bad)peor (worse)

Adverbs

PositiveComparative

poco (little)menos (less)

mucho (much)más (more)

mal (badly)peor (worse)

bien (well)mejor (better)

CHAPTER 12: CONVERSATIONAL PHRASES

TALKING ABOUT YOURSELF

Knowing how to introduce and tell something about yourself is one of the basic skills you should acquire when learning a new language.

Here is an example:

Me llamo John Vasquez. Nací el 12 de enero de 1985. Tengo treinta y dos años cumplidos. Trabajo como enfermero en Hospital de XYZ. Vivo en Nueva York pero soy de Barcelona, España. Estoy casado con dos hijos. Tengo dos hermanos y una hermana. Mi padre es abogado mientras que mi madre es un médico. Mis pasatiempos son jugar al tenis y dibujar.

My name is John Vasquez. I was born on January 12, 1985. I am thirty-two years old. I work as a nurse in XYZ Hospital. I live in New York but I'm from Barcelona, Spain. I'm married with two kids. I have two brothers and a sister. My father is a lawyer while my mother is a doctor. My hobbies are playing tennis and sketching.

INTRODUCTIONS

If you want to meet new people and make Spanish-speaking friends, you should know how to introduce yourself properly to avoid awkward situations.

In general, the formal way of addressing people is used when meeting someone for the first time.

To ask for someone's name, you would say:

¿Cómo se llama usted? What's your name?

KOH-moh say YAHM-ah oo-STED

The informal form may be appropriate if you're talking to someone who is obviously younger, like a child, or a pet:

¿Cómo te llamas?What's your name?

KOH-mo tay YAHM-ahss

To reply and introduce yourself, you can use any of the following phrases:

Mi nombre es _______.My name is ________.

Me llamo __________.My name is ________.

may YAHM-oh

It is customary to express your pleasure at the introduction. Here are the acceptable phrases:

¡Muchísimo gusto!I'm very pleased to meet you!

¡Mucho gusto!I'm pleased to meet you!

¡Tanto Gusto!Nice to meet you!

If you want to know more about the person, you may ask him or her some questions such as the following:

Formal

¿Donde vive?Where do you live?

¿De dónde es usted?Where are you from?

¿Está usted casado/casada?Are you married?

¿Cuando es su cumpleaños?When is your birthday?

¿Cuántos años tiene?How old are you?

¿Cuál es su edad?What is your age?

Familiar:

¿Donde vives?Where do you live?

¿De dónde eres?Where are you from?

¿Estás casado/casada?Are you married?

¿Cuando es tu cumpleaños?When is your birthday?

¿Cuántos años tienes?How old are you?

Take note that it is generally considered rude to ask about someone's age.

You can use the following phrases to respond:

Soy de los Estados Unidos.

I'm from the United States.

Vivo en Chicago.

I live in Chicago.

Tengo veintiocho años.

I'm twenty-eight years old.

Mi cumpleaños es el 25 de marzo.

My birthday is on March 25.

No, estoy soltero/soltera.

No, I am a bachelor/bachelorette.

Si, estoy casado/casada.

Yes, I am married.

To introduce a third person, you can use these phrases:

To introduce your spouse:

Esta es mi esposa, Lolita.This is my wife, Lolita.

Este es mi marido, Arturo.This is my husband, Arturo.

To introduce a friend:

Se llama Martha.Her name is Martha.

Ells es de Texas.She is from Texas.

Este es mi amigo, Mario.This is my friend, Mario.

Es un escritor.He is a writer.

THE FAMILY

Learning the names for each member of the family is one of the intial steps that you should take in your language learning journey. Knowing how to call your parents, spouse, brothers, sisters, and other relatives will help you learn to talk about your family.

Here is a vocabulary list for the members of the family:

los padres	parents
el padre	father
la madre	mother
los abuelos	grandparents
la abuela	grandmother
el abuelo	grandfather
el marido	husband
la esposa	wife
la hija	daughter
el hijo	son
el nieto	grandson
la nieta	granddaughter
el ahijado	grandson
la ahijada	granddaughter
la hermana	sister
el hermano	brother
el hermano mayor	older brother
la hermana mayor	older sister
el hermano menor	younger brother
la hermana menor	younger sister
el hermanito	baby brother
la hermanita	baby sister
el medio	half brother

hermano	
la media hermana	half sister
la tía	aunt
el tío	uncle
los primos	cousins
el primo	male cousin
la prima	female cousin
la sobrina	niece
el sobrino	nephew
la suegra	mother-in-law
el suegro	father-in-law
la cuñada	sister-in-law
el cuñado	brother-in-law
el yerno	son-in-law
la nuera	daughter-in-law
los hijastrados	stepchildren
el hermanastro	stepbrother
la hermanastra	stepsister

PARTS OF THE HOUSE

The house is where you spend most of your time. Hence, you should familiarize yourself with the vocabulary words for each part of the house as well as the objects inside or around it.

These are the names of the rooms:

la habitaciónroom

el dormitoriobedroom

el salonliving room

la cocinakitchen

el comedordining room

el despachostudy

cuarto para visitasguest room

el cuarto de bañobathroom

el cuarto del bebébaby's room

la despensapantry

lavanderíalaundry room

el aseotoilet

The other parts of the house are:

la cocheragarage

el sótanobasement

la chimeneafireplace

el balcónbalcony

el pasillohall

el techoceiling

la paredwall

el suelofloor

el jardíngarden

la terrazaterrace

las escalerasstairs

el ascensorelevator

el céspedlawn

la puertadoor

la ventanawindow

el portalporch

el desvánloft

el tejadoroof

calefacción centralcentral heating

abajodownstairs

arribaupstairs

TALKING ABOUT THE WEATHER (EL TIEMPO)

Asking someone about the weather is a common way of starting a conversation.

The following questions are used to find out what the weather is:

¿Qué tiempo hace?

¿Cómo está el tiempo?

They are both translated as "How's the weather?".

You can also say "¿Cómo está el clima?" which means "How's the weather/climate?"

Alternatively, you can ask:

"¿Cómo está por afuera?" which means "What is it like outside?"

The verbs hacer, estar, and haber are used to express weather conditions.

These expressions tell something about the weather:

Hace buen tiempo.The weather is good.

Hace mal tiempo.The weather is bad.

Hace sol.It's sunny.

Hace viento.It's windy.

Hay niebla.It is foggy.

Hace frío.It's cold.

Hace calor.It's hot.

Está nevando.It is snowing.

Está lloviendo.It is raining.

Llueve.It rains.

Nieva.It snows.

Brilla el sol.The sun shines.

The following are the most common weather terms:

una brisa	a breeze
un cielo despejado	a clear sky
un chaparrón	a cloudburst
un frente frío	a cold front
un turbión	a downpour
un relámpago	a flash of lightning
una inundación	a flood
una racha	a gust of wind
una granizada	a hailstorm

una ola de calor	a heat wave
una brisa marina	a sea breeze
una bola de nieve	a snowball
una tormenta	a storm
un día soleado	a sunny day
un claro	a sunny spell
un trueno	a thunderclap
un nubarrón	a thundercloud
borrascoso	blustery
una nube	cloud
húmedo	damp
el rocío	dew
llovizna	drizzle
una culebrina	forked lightning
escarcha	frost
húmedo	humid
la humedad	humidity
un huracán	hurricane
la neblina	mist
el sereno	night dew
la lluvia	rain
chubascos aislados	scattered showers
la bruma	sea mist
aguanieve	sleet
chubascos de aguanieve	sleet showers
la nieve	snow
chubascos de nieve	snow showers
el sol	sun
el litoral	the coastal area
los truenos	thunder
nevar	to snow
deshelar	to thaw
la turbulencia	turbulence
el viento	wind

Greetings And Common Expressions

English	Spanish
Good morning!	¡Buenos días!
Good afternoon!	¡Buenas tardes!
Good evening!	¡Buenas noches!
Hello! (informal)	Hola!
See you tomorrow.	Hasta mañana.
See you soon.	Hasta pronto.
See you.	Hasta la vista.
See you later.	Hasta luego.
We'll see you!	¡Nos vemos!
Have a nice day!	¡Que le vaya bien!
Good luck!	¡Buena suerte!
Goodbye.	Adiós.
Welcome!	¡Bienvenidos!
Congratulations!	¡Felicitaciones!
Bless you!	¡Salud!
I'm sorry.	Lo siento.
Thank you (very much).	(Muchas) Gracias.
You're welcome.	De nada.
Please.	Por favor.
I love you.	Te amo.
How are you? (inf)	¿Cómo estás?
How are you? (formal)	¿Cómo está usted?
How's it going?	¿Qué tal?
Very good.	Muy bien .
That's alright.	Está bien.
Yes.	Sí.
No.	No.
Sure.	Claro.
Of course.	Claro que sí.
Mister	Señor

Mrs.	Señora
Miss	Señorita
What's happening?	¿Qué pasa?
Maybe.	Quizás.
It depends.	Depende.
Ready?	¿Listo?
I'm hungry.	Tengo hambre.
I'm thirsty.	Tengo sed.
I'm cold.	Tengo frío.
I'm hot.	Tengo calor.
I forgot.	Me olvidé.
Not yet.	Todavía no.
Good idea!	¡Buena idea!
What is that?	¿Qué es eso?
There is/are ___.	Hay ___
There was/were ___.	Había ___
Here	Aquí
There	Ahí
Can you help me? (formal)	¿Puede ayudarme?
Do you understand? (formal)	¿Entiende usted?
Do you understand? (informal)	¿Entiendes?
Help!	¡Ayuda!
I'm sick.	Estoy enfermo.
I don't know.	No lo sé.
I understand.	Entiendo.
I don't understand.	No Entiendo.
How much is this?	¿Cuánto cuesta?

Spanish Short Stories

"Sueños/Dreams"

Carlos llevó a su hijo a la plaza. Era algo que solían disfrutar los dos cuando hacía buen tiempo. En el medio del parque, había una estatua de bronce de un soldado mirando hacia el horizonte. Debajo de él, había una placa que decía "Sargento Gómez falleció aquí en 1880 luchando por lo que es correcto".

Mientras su hijo jugaba en el arenero, Carlos miraba profundamente a la estatua. Siempre sintió una especie de conexión con ese sargento, aun cuando él llevaba años muerto, y no tenía ninguna conexión familiar. Pero había algo en esa estatua que le llamaba la atención, y no podía decir qué era.

Esa noche, Carlos, luego de cocinarle a su hijo su comida favorita, decidió acostarlo, y luego ver un poco de televisión. Cambió los canales, y en uno de ellos, encontró un documental sobre la guerra de la Independencia. De pronto, el sueño y el cansancio lo vencieron, y se quedó profundamente dormido.

En su sueño, se encontraba en una especie de campo de combate lleno de barro. Había caballos, explosiones y gente corriendo y gritando. De pronto, una explosión lo tiró al piso y lo dejó aturdido. Carlos tenía miedo, todo parecía muy real, y no podía entender qué es lo que estaba pasando.

Muchacho, arriba, levántese, que tenemos que seguir combatiendo – Una voz amable pero firme sonó detrás de él.

Carlos se dio vuelta y logró ver al Sargento Gómez mirándolo fijamente, con la misma seguridad que tendría en su estatua muchos años después. Como pudo, Carlos se levantó. El Sargento apoyó la mano en su espalda, y le dijo:

Vamos. No me decepcione, que la muerte todavía no nos va a conquistar hoy.

Sorprendido y asustado, Carlos se despertó. Tenía una sensación rara en su cuerpo, como si el sueño hubiera sido real. Trató de olvidarlo, pero no pudo lograrlo. Apagó la televisión, y se dirigió al baño para asearse y prepararse para ir a dormir. En el espejo, vio su reflejo y le sorprendió notar que su cara se encontraba llena de barro. Miró a su alrededor, y notó de que sus zapatos también tenían barro. Pero fue un sueño, no puede haber sido verdad.

Quizás…

Questionnaire

- What was Carlos doing in the park?
- Do you have a park close by? If the answer is yes, does it have a statue in the center?
- Have you ever had a dream like Carlos had? What happened?
- In five or six sentences, try to change the ending of the story. Remember, do it in Spanish, and then in English, just to be sure that you understand the vocabulary used.

Let's review some grammar and fun facts!

"Plaza" and "park" are the same word, and in Spanish, they are translated to plaza and parque respectively.

In most countries and main cities, you will find statues and big parks around them. It's very common to see families enjoying their day, reading, or playing football.

Translation

Carlos took his son to the park. It was something that they both used to enjoy when the weather was good. In the center of the park, there was a bronze statue of a soldier watching the horizon. Underneath, there was a plaque that said "Sergent Gomez passed away here in 1880 fighting for what was right."

While his son played in the sandbox, Carlos looked deeply to the statue. He always felt some sort of connection with that sergeant, even though he has been dead for years, and he had no family connection with him. But there was something in that statue that drew attention, and he couldn't say what it was.

That night, Carlos, after cooking his son his favorite food, decided to put him down, and then watch some television. Changed the channels, and, in one of them, he found a documentary about the Independence War. Suddenly, sleep and fatigue defeated him, and he fell profoundly asleep.

In his dream, he found himself in some sort of a combat field full of mud. There were horses, explosions and people running and shouting. Suddenly, an explosion took him to the floor and left him stunned. Carlos was afraid, everything seemed so real, and he couldn't understand what was happening.

> "Lad, up, get up, we have to keep fighting." A kind but firm voice sounded behind him.

Carlos turned around and managed to see Sargent Gomez watching him fiercely, with the same certainty that his statue will have many years later. As he could, Carlos got up. The Sargent put his hand over his back and said,

"Let's go. Don't let me down, Death will not conquer us today."

Surprised and scared, Carlos woke up. He had a weird feeling in his body like the dream was way too real. He tried to forget, but he couldn't make it. Turned off the television, and went to the bathroom to clean himself up and prepare to go to bed. In the mirror, he saw his reflection and was surprised to note that his face was full of mud. Looked around, and realized that his shoes were also full of mud. But it was a dream, it couldn't be true.

Maybe…

"El último Hombre/The Last Man"

Miguel se despertó esa mañana repentinamente. Estaba llegando tarde a clases, ya la tercera vez esa semana. No podía ser, si había puesto la alarma correctamente. Se vistió rápidamente, tomó su mochila, y salió corriendo de su casa.

Al llegar a la esquina, notó algo raro: No había nadie en la calle. No solamente gente, sino también autos o animales. Ni siquiera se escuchaban los sonidos de la construcción que estaba a una cuadra de su hogar. Había un absoluto silencio. Extrañado, y un poco asustado, Miguel comenzó a caminar hacia el colegio. No había nadie, y según su reloj, ya debería haber estudiantes en clases. Donde fuera que caminara, no había nadie. ¿Será algún tipo de broma? ¿Algo pasó mientras dormía? ¿Qué es lo que había pasado?

Miguel era fanático de la ciencia ficción, y lo primero que pensó era que toda la gente había sido raptada por extraterrestres. Pero claro, no tenía sentido, porque los extraterrestres no existen. Continuó caminando por todos lados, ya bastante desesperado de que fuera el último hombre sobre la Tierra. Entró a cines, autos abandonados, donde fuera que pudiera encontrar gente, pero no había nadie. Era como si nadie hubiera existido jamás.

A la distancia, un ser extraño lo miraba con sus diez ojos. Extendió sus tentáculos, y estableció conexión con la madre nodriza a través del pensamiento.

Nos olvidamos de un humano. XCY24 hará contacto y lo eliminará.

Miguel llegó a ver una luz violeta detrás de él, y luego nada más. Al menos no sintió dolor.

QUESTIONNAIRE

- Have you ever been late to class? What happened?
- Do you live far away from your work?
- If you woke up and found yourself the last human on Earth, what would you do? (I personally would use that time to read all kinds of books!)
- What do you think happened to all the pets and animals?

Let's review some grammar and fun facts!

One example, that we will expand in the next chapter, of words that have two meanings is *"theater."* In Spanish, it can be translated as *teatro* (where you go to see plays from Shakespeare and the like) or as *cine* (where you go to watch movies).

When you are in doubt about what it means, try to search for clues in the context. Most of the time, you can infer the word by looking at the context. But if by any chance you can't do it, and it's a conversation that you are having with someone, ask him what he meant.

TRANSLATION

Miguel suddenly woke up that morning. He was late for classes, the third time that week. That couldn't happen if he had set up the alarm correctly. He dressed up quickly, took his backup and left his house running.

When he reached the corner, he noticed something really strange: There was nobody in the street. Not just people, but also cars or animals. Not even the sounds of the construction a block from his house could be heard. There was an absolute silence. Amazed, and a bit scared, Miguel started walking to the school. There was nobody there, and according to his watch, there should be some students in the class. Wherever he walked, there was nobody. Is this some kind of joke? Something happened while he was sleeping? What has happened?

Miguel was a science fiction fan, and the first thing he thought was that all the people were kidnapped by aliens. But, of course, it didn't make sense, because aliens don't exist. He continued walking everywhere, already really desperate that he was the last man on Earth. He went into movie theatres, abandoned cars, wherever that he might find people, but there was nobody there. It was like no one has ever existed.

In the distance, a strange being watched him with its ten eyes. It extended its tentacles and established a connection with the mothership through its thought.

"We forgot one human. XCY24 shall make contact and eliminate him."

Miguel saw a purple light behind him, and nothing else. At least he didn't feel pain.

"Mala Suerte/Bad Luck"

Esteban tomaba el subterráneo todos los días a la misma hora. Durante su viaje, siempre se encontraba con las mismas personas: Mario y Lucía. Ellos eran una pareja amable, que llevaban saliendo alrededor de 5 años. Todas las mañanas, ellos compartían el viaje hacia el centro de la ciudad, y luego, cada uno se dividía para ir a sus trabajos. Esteban trabajaba como diseñador de interiores en una empresa multinacional, mientras que Mario trabajaba en sistemas programando servidores y conexiones de telefonía, y Lucía era maestra de primaria en una escuela cercana.

Un día, Esteban estaba un poco deprimido. Había intentado tener una cita la última semana, pero la realidad es que no fue muy interesante. La chica era de la misma edad que Esteban, pero al llegar al restaurante, ella no dejó de usar el celular en ningún momento. Cuando Esteban intentaba hablar o hacerle alguna pregunta personal, ella contestaba que estaba ocupada, y seguía usando el teléfono. Al final, Esteban decidió pagar la cuenta, e irse temprano a casa. Cuando le dijo esto a la muchacha, no parecía que le importaba mucho.

Bueno, Esteban, tú no tienes suerte con las relaciones, ¿eh? – Dijo Mario, al escuchar la historia al día siguiente.

Sí – Contestó – Creo que voy a morir solo y triste.

¡Vamos, no digas eso! – Le recriminó Lucía – Mira, tengo una propuesta que capaz te interesa. Quiero que vengas a nuestra casa a cenar mañana a la noche.

No sé – comentó triste Esteban – Me parece que tengo planes.

¿Qué planes? ¿Jugar videojuegos toda la noche?

Bueno, es un plan humilde…

Vas a venir, y te aviso, no tomo un no como respuesta.

Al día siguiente, Esteban se debatió mucho entre ir o mentir y decir que estaba enfermo. Al final, decidió bañarse, vestirse e ir. Después de todo, no tenía mucho que perder, y además, él estaba seguro que una fiesta no cambiaría absolutamente nada de su situación. Al llegar, tocó el timbre y esperó. Sintió los pasos detrás de la puerta, y cuando se abrió, se quedó completamente sorprendido: En lugar de que lo recibiera Mario o Lucía, había una mujer pelirroja, con un largo vestido que le llegaba hasta las rodillas, y una sonrisa que inmediatamente lo cautivó.

Perdón, creo que… marqué el timbre equivocado – tartamudeó Esteban

¿Viene a la fiesta de Lucía? Sí, es aquí. Vamos, pasa. Tú debes ser Esteban.

Sí, sí, ¿y tú?

Mi nombre es Andrea, soy una compañera de trabajo de Lucía.

La siguió dentro de la casa, aún sorprendido por la belleza de Andrea. Cuando ingresó al comedor, se encontraban sus amigos esperándolo, ambos con una sonrisa enorme. Mario, al ver la cara de sorpresa de Esteban, no pudo evitar largar una carcajada, que luego tuvo que excusar que era porque se había acordado de un chiste que le habían contado en la semana. Todos se sentaron a comer, y mientras Lucía servía la comida, Mario le hacía preguntas a Esteban sobre su trabajo.

¿Y qué tal te fue en el último proyecto que trabajaste? – Y luego, mirando a Andrea, añadió – Esteban es diseñador de interiores, y la semana pasada nos comentó que estaba trabajando en la reformación de las galerías que se encuentran cerca del museo.

Bueno, eh, no es tan importante como parece – Tímidamente respondió Esteban – Estamos tratando de lograr hacer que esas galerías se puedan utilizar nuevamente, y para esto, bueno, estamos reformando las estructuras y la pintura.

¡Eso suena genial! – Dijo Andrea – A mi novio le encantará saber todo sobre eso.

Se hizo un profundo silencio en la mesa. Lucía la miró con dudas.

Pero… me habías dicho que estabas soltera.

Ah, sí, pero es que nos reconciliamos, y decidimos volver a intentar de nuevo una relación. De todas maneras, no creí que fuera necesario aclararlo. ¿Acaso me invitaste a cenar porque querías que lo conociera a tu amigo?

Sí, de hecho, fue mi idea – Dijo Mario, tratando de calmar la situación – No pensamos que estabas saliendo con alguien – Y mirando a Esteban, añadió – Te pido disculpas.

La cena prosiguió bastante normal. Esteban ayudó a lavar los platos, y cuando estaba por salir, Andrea le pidió si no la podía acompañar mientras esperaba un taxi.

Afuera, ambos comenzaron a conversar.

Sabes… No quiero que sientas que no tendría nada contigo – Dijo Andrea

Entiendo. De todas maneras, la verdad es que la cena fue bastante buena, y con eso me quedo contento.

¿Es cierto que haces diseño de interiores? Porque creo que te puedo ofrecer algo que te gustará.

Por favor, que no sea otro encuentro forzado – Sonrió Esteban. A pesar de todo, le gustaba hablar con ella.

No, no – contestó entre risas- Nada parecido a eso. Toma mi tarjeta, y llámame. Ah, y una cosa más… Realmente me haces reír mucho. ¿Te parece que hablemos para juntarnos en una semana o dos?

Llegó un taxi, y se despidieron rápidamente. Esteban se quedó mirando la tarjeta, pensativo. Bueno, al menos tenía una amiga nueva. Después de todo, no fue una mala idea haber salido de casa.

QUESTIONNAIRE

- Have you ever had bad luck at a date? What happened?
- Do you have any good friends like Mario and Lucía?
- Write down, in a few sentences, if you had a bad date, and if you did, what you did to change it. Remember, in Spanish!

Let's review some grammar and fun facts!

"Date" in English means two things, but the fun thing in Spanish is that the word also has two meanings in Spanish:

"Date" can be translated as *fecha* (a date, for example, July 10th) or as a *cita* ("Juan and Carlos go out on a date").

There are a lot of words that in Spanish have two meanings. I will give you an example:

muñeca – Doll/Wrist

nada – Swim/Nothing

There are a couple of good jokes about it, for example, the one my daughter always tells me and laughs:

- Un pez se encuentra con otro, y le pregunta qué hace su papá.
- Nada.

The rough translation would be (and keep in mind that in Spanish it's hilarious, but in English it loses some of the charm):

"One fish meets another one, and asks what does his father do."

"Nothing/Swim."

See? There are a lot of words in Spanish that have two meanings. That's why Spanish is fantastic for double entendre jokes.

TRANSLATION

Esteban takes the subway every day at the hour. During his trip, he always met with the same people: Mario and Lucía. They were a nice couple, who has been going out for the past five years. Every morning, they shared the ride to the center of the city, and then, they each went their own ways to their jobs. Esteban worked as an interior designer for a multinational company, while Mario worked in IT programming servers and network connections, and Lucía was a primary school teacher in a school nearby.

One day, Esteban was a bit depressed. He had tried to have a date the past week, but the reality was that it wasn't very interesting. The girl was the same age as Esteban, but after arriving at the restaurant, she didn't stop using her cell phone at any time. When Esteban tried to talk or ask her any personal question, she answered that she was busy, and continued using her phone. In the end, Esteban decided to pay the bill and go home early that night. When he mentioned this to the girl, it didn't seem like she cared.

> "Well, Esteban, you don't have any luck with relationships, eh?" said Mario after listening to the story the next day.
>
> "Yeah," he replied. "I believe that I will die alone and sad."
>
> "C'mon, don't say that!" Lucía reproached him. "Look, I have a proposition that might interest you. I want you to come over to our house for dinner tomorrow night."
>
> "I don't know, said Esteban sadly. "I believe that I have other plans."
>
> "What plans? Playing video games all night?"
>
> "Well, it's a humble plan…"
>
> "You are going to come, and I warn you, I don't take a no for an answer."

The next day, Esteban really debated himself between going, or lying and saying he was sick. In the end, he decided to take a shower, get dressed and go. After all, he didn't have much to lose, and also, he was sure that a party wouldn't change absolutely anything of his situation. When he arrived, he rang the doorbell and waited. He heard the steps behind the door, and when it opened, he was absolutely surprised: In place of there being Mario or Lucía, there was a redheaded woman, with a long dress that got to her knees, and a smile that immediately captivated him.

> "Sorry, I think that… I rang the wrong doorbell," Esteban stuttered.
>
> "Are you coming to Lucía's party? Yeah, it's here. C'mon, get in. You must be Esteban."
>
> "Yeah…yeah, and you?"
>
> "My name is Andrea, I'm a work colleague of Lucía's."

He followed her into the house, still surprised by Andrea's beauty. When he entered the dining room, he found his friends waiting for him, both with a huge smile. Mario, when he saw Esteban's surprised face, couldn't suppress a fit of laughter, that then he had to excuse himself saying that he had remembered a joke that he heard during the week. Everybody sat down to dinner, and while Lucía served the food, Mario asked questions Esteban about his work.

> "And how did it go in the last project that you worked on?" And then, watching Andrea, added, "Esteban is an interior designer, and the past week told us that he was working on the reforms of the galleries close to the museum."

"Well, eh, it's not as important as it sounds, timidly, Esteban replied. "We are trying to make it so those galleries can be used again, and for this, we are reforming the structures and painting."

"That sounds great!" Andrea said. "My boyfriend would love to hear everything about that."

A deep silence falls over the table. Lucía looked at her dubiously…

"But… You said that you were single."

"Ah, yeah, but it happened that we got back together, and decided to try a relationship again. Anyway, I didn't think that it was necessary to clarify that. By any chance, did you invite me to dinner because you wanted me to meet your friend?"

"Yeah, in fact, it was my idea," Mario said, trying to calm the situation. "We didn't think that you were dating someone." And looking at Esteban, he added,"I apologize."

The dinner proceeded pretty normally. Esteban helped to wash the dinner plates, and when he was about to go, Andrea asked him if he couldn't be with her while she waited for a cab.

Outside, both started to talk:

"You know, I don't want you to feel that I wouldn't have anything to do with you," Andrea said.

"I understand. In any case, the truth is that the dinner was pretty good, and with that I'm happy."

"Is true that you do interior design? Because I think that I can offer you something that you might like."

"Please, let itnot be another forced encounter." Esteban smiled. Despite everything, he enjoyed talking to her.

"No, no," she answered while laughing. "Nothing like that. Take my card, and call me. Ah, and one other thing… You really make me laugh. How about that we talk so we can meet in a week or two?"

A cab arrived, and they quickly said goodbye. Esteban stayed looking at the card, thoughtful. Well, at least he had a new friend. After all, it hadn't been a bad idea to leave the house.

"El viaje a las Ruinas de los Incas/The trip to the Ruins of the Incas"

Todavía recuerdo la primera vez que realmente pensé en ser arqueólogo. Tenía 10 años y mi padre me había prometido que iba a llevarme al cine si aprobaba todas mis materias. Estudié esa semana como nunca había estudiado antes, y, llegado la hora de los exámenes, los aprobé todos con una excelente nota. Siempre fiel a su palabra, papá me llevó al cine del barrio. Ahí fue cuando vi por primera vez Indiana Jones y Los Cazadores del Arca Perdida. Mientras miraba a Harrison Ford saltando, golpeando a los villanos, encontrando las pistas que lo llevarían a encontrar el Arca de la Alianza, algo dentro mío cambió para siempre: Quería ser él. Quería tener esas aventuras, enamorarme de ese tipo de mujeres, vivir al máximo.

Al llegar a casa, atormenté a mi padre con preguntas. ¿Cómo podía ser arqueólogo? ¿Había que estudiar mucho? ¿Dónde había que estudiar? ¿Qué pasos tenía que seguir?. Mi padre adoptó una actitud que voy a valorar el resto de mi vida, y comenzó a conseguir información al respecto. Él no sabía cómo se estudiaba eso, después de todo, era simplemente un obrero que nunca pudo terminar la secundaria. Pero al ver mis ojos brillando ante la posibilidad de ser como Indiana Jones, él hizo todo lo que se encontraba en sus manos (y aún mucho más) para darme todas las chances necesarias de cumplir mis sueños. Trabajó horas extras, organizamos salidas a la biblioteca para poder leer todo lo que fuera remotamente parecido a la arqueología, me compraba revistas de ciencia e investigación, recortaba partes del periódico donde se detallaban expediciones o avances científicos en la exploración de las pirámides. Incluso logró obtener la dirección de correo postal de un famoso arqueólogo de mi país, y me insistió en que le escriba una carta.

En la carta, le pregunté absolutamente de todo, desde cuáles eran sus teorías sobre quién construyó las pirámides, hasta sobre cuál era la mejor manera de usar un látigo. Quería saberlo todo. La respuesta de la carta tardó un poco en llegar. Cuando lo hizo, 3 meses después de que yo la había enviado, fue un poco escueta. Pero la primera línea de la carta fue lo que más me llamó la atención:

> "Disculpa porque no pude contestar antes, pero es que estaba de viaje en Egipto.
>
> Aparentemente, hay una tumba que no podemos explicar el origen"

¡Egipto! ¡Estuvo en Egipto! El resto de la carta eran consejos sobre qué carrera estudiar, y dónde era el mejor lugar para hacerlo. Abracé a mi papá, con lágrimas en los ojos, y le agradecí todo el esfuerzo que hizo para conseguirme esto. De más está decir que ese día los dos lloramos abrazados, y decidimos darnos un gusto comiendo un poco de helado.

Varios años después, me gradué de arqueólogo de la universidad más prestigiosa de mi país, y si bien mi padre había fallecido un par de años antes por culpa de una enfermedad, no podía dejar de sentir una tristeza, pero a la vez felicidad porque logré cumplir la meta que me había puesto desde tan chico. Al poco tiempo de haberme graduado, me ofrecieron un puesto importante de investigación en la Universidad de Oxford.

¡No lo podía creer! Tanto esfuerzo finalmente había rendido frutos. Así que empaqué, y me dirigí hacia Oxford, lugar de mi próxima aventura. Me dieron una oficina, un asistente con el que tenía que trabajar, e incluso me ofrecieron la posibilidad de dar clases. ¿Yo, dando clases de arqueología? No lo podía creer, todo esto era mucho para mí, era como un sueño y yo seguía dormido. Así que la realidad de mi trabajo diario fue la primera que me golpeó en la cara. Todo el día encerrado en una oficina, corrigiendo exámenes, leyendo informes y trabajos de mis alumnos. ¿Dónde estaban mis viajes por las junglas de Sudamérica? ¿Dónde estaban mis villanos muy malos, y las reliquias muy viejas? ¿Acaso era todo mentira?

Decidí juntar dinero, y para mis siguientes vacaciones, irme a explorar las ruinas de los Incas. Subí a un avión, y cuando llegué allá, lo primero que hice fue anotarme en una excursión para visitar las ruinas. Llegué ahí, con mi cincel y un diario para tomar nota, esperando encontrarme con algo que nadie había explorado, con alguna reliquia perdida que había sido ignorada. Pero estaba lleno de turistas con cámaras de fotos, dejando rastros de basura por todos lados. ¿Acaso no entendían que eso podía perjudicar cualquier exploración del lugar que uno quisiera llevar a cabo? Traté de escapar de la multitud de turistas, y me adentré en un camino que decía "Prohibido pasar". Pisé un cúmulo de hojas que parecían haber quedado del anterior otoño, y el suelo se abrió y me envolvió en una profunda oscuridad. Caí en lo que parecía ser un pozo.

Tomé mi encendedor, y lo usé para iluminarme. No había ningún rastro de nada. Era un pozo sin ningún tipo de marca, ni pintura, ni tampoco alguna manera de salir de ahí. Grité y grité, pero nadie logró escucharme. El hambre me hacía doler el estómago, y mis costillas parecían fracturadas, a juzgar por el dolor que sentía. Comencé incluso a dejar de sentir mis extremidades. Hasta que una luz me envolvió, y una voz muy familiar me llamó por mi nombre.

Ven. Ya pasó todo. Ya estás bien. Toma, te traje un poco de helado.

QUESTIONNAIRE

- What is your favorite movie? Why?
- Have you ever seen any of the Indiana Jones movies?
- Have you ever visited Oxford or do you know someone who studied there?
- Write down a different ending, where the main character, instead of falling into a well, finds an old relic.

Let's review some grammar and fun facts!

In Spanish, funnily enough, the name Indiana Jones isn't translated because names aren't translated for the most part. Juan would be Juan in English, although some people prefer it to translate it anyway. For example:

Juan – John

Carlos – Charles

Susana – Susan

Lucía - Lucy

But some names stay the same:

David

Andrea

Bianca

Bruno

TRANSLATION

I still remember the first time that I really thought to be an archaeologist.

I was 10 years old and my father had promised me that he would take me to the movie theater only if I passed all my subjects. I studied that week like I never had before, and, when the exams came, I passed them all with excellent marks.

Always loyal to his word, Dad took me to my neighborhood cinema. It was where I saw for the first time Indiana Jones and the Raiders of the Lost Ark. While I was watching Harrison Ford jumping, punching the bad guys, finding clues that will help him to find the Ark of the Covenant, something inside me changed forever: I wanted to be him. I wanted to have those adventures, fall in love with that kind of woman, live fully.

When I arrived home, I tormented my father with questions. How could I be an archaeologist? Do I have to study a lot? Where should I study? What steps should I follow? My father adopted an attitude that I will appreciate the rest of my life and started to get information on the subject.

He didn't know where to study that. After all, he was just a worker who never finished high school. But when he saw my eyes shining before the possibility of being like Indiana Jones, he did whateverhe could (and even more) to give me every necessary chance to fulfill my dreams.

He worked overtime, we organized trips to the library in order to read everything that had a remote connection with archaeology, he bought me science and research magazines, he cut articles from the newspaper where expeditions or scientific advances in the exploration of the pyramids were mentioned.

He even managed to obtain the postal address of a famous archaeologist of my country, and he insisted I write him a letter.

In the letter, I asked him absolutely everything, from what his theories were about who built the pyramids, to what the best way was to use a whip. I wanted to know everything.

The answer to the letter took a while to arrive. When it did, three months after I had sent it, it was a bit succinct. But the first line of the letter was what jumped to my attention:

"Sorry that I couldn't reply before, but I was on a trip in Egypt.

Apparently, there is a tomb and we can't explain its origin."

Egypt! He was in Egypt! The rest of the letter was advice over what career to study, and where it was the best place to do it. I hugged my Dad, with tears in my eyes, and I thanked everything he did to get this for me. It goes without saying that we both cried while hugging that day, and we decided to get a treat, a bit of ice cream.

Several years later, I graduated as an archaeologist from the most prestigious university in my country, and while my father had passed away a couple of years before because of a sickness, I couldn't stop feeling sad, but at the same time happy because I finally was able to fulfill the goal that I decided when I was a kid. Soon after graduating, I was offered an important research job at the University of Oxford.

I couldn't believe it! So much effort had finally paid off. So I packed up and went to Oxford, the place of my next adventure.

They gave me an office, an assistant with I could work with, and they even offered me the possibility to teach. Me? Teaching archaeology? I couldn't believe it, this was too much for me, it was like a dream and I was still sleeping.

So the reality of my daily job was the first to hit me in my face. All day locked up in an office, grading exams, reading reports and work from my students. Where were the trips through the jungles of South America? Where were the really bad guys, and the really old relics? Was it all a lie?

I decided to save up some money, and for my next vacations, I went to explore the ruins of the Incas.

I got up on a plane, and when I got there, the first thing that I did was to sign up to an excursion to visit the ruins. I arrived there, with my chisel and a diary to take notes, expecting to find something that no one has ever explored before, with old lost relics that had been ignored.

But it was full of tourists with cameras, leaving trash everywhere. Did they not understand that it could harm any exploration of the place that one might want to perform?

I tried to escape the crowd of tourists, and went into a road that said, "Do not enter." I step over a cluster of leaves that were there from the past autumn, and the floor opened and swallowed me in a deep darkness. I fell in what it looked like a well.

I took my lighter and used it to illuminate my surroundings. There wasn't a sign of anything. It was a well without any kind of mark, paint or any way to get out. I screamed and screamed, but no one could hear me. Hunger made my stomach hurt, and my ribs seemed broken, judging by the pain that I felt. I started to even stop feeling my arms and legs.

Until a light enveloped me, and a very familiar voice called me by my name.

"Come. It's all over. You are all right now. Here, I brought you some ice cream."

"El Tatuaje Viviente / The Living Tattoo"

Finalmente llevé a cabo la tontera más grande de mi vida. Amigos y familiares me dijeron que no lo haga, incluso mi propia consciencia me insistió que no lo haga. Pero me decidí: Me hice un tatuaje.

Elegirlo no fue fácil. Al principio pensé en hacer algo alegórico a mis gatitos, quizás una patita o algo que me recuerde lo mucho que los quiero. Pero luego, cuando comencé a ver diseños, noté que mucha gente se hacía eso, y la verdad es que no quería seguir la corriente de lo que hacen las otras personas. Siempre me definí como una chica bastante singular y especial, así que lo que menos quería era hacer era seguir la corriente.

Mi búsqueda me llevó a encontrar símbolos tribales, similares a los que tenía mi entrenador personal en el gimnasio. Esos me gustaron mucho más, pero otra vez, mis búsquedas me mostraron que todo el mundo usaba algo parecido. Ya cerca de la frustración y a punto de olvidarme de mi capricho, encontré finalmente lo que quería: Dos estrellas rodeando un animalito dentro. ¡Me encantó! Me parecía muy tierno, y si lograba cambiar y hacer que el tatuador ponga a mis gatitos, iba a quedar muchísimo mejor.

Luego de elegir el diseño, llegó el momento de encontrar el mejor precio para alguien que tiene un presupuesto chico como yo. Cada uno de los tatuadores que visité me pedían una fortuna para lograrlo, y yo no entendía por qué. Después de todo, son simplemente un par de líneas, un poco de dibujo, color, sombras, también adaptar la cara de mis bebés al tatuaje, y por supuesto, hacerlo todo rápido y que quede perfecto. No puede costar tanto.

Por suerte, encontré en un barrio abandonado, cerca de un cementerio, en un día donde llovía muchísimo, y sólo pude darme cuenta porque un trueno iluminó el cartel que indicaba que había un tatuador que cobraba poco dinero por su trabajo. ¡Qué casualidad! Cuando entro, el tatuador me mira fijamente. Tenía una barba larga, y una mirada penetrante. Me miró de arriba abajo, y me preguntó si quería un tatuaje.

¿Cómo supo eso?

Porque soy un tatuador. La gente no entra acá buscando información de los partidos de fútbol.

Ah, claro – Contesté- ¿Puede tatuarme este dibujito, pero con unos gatitos?

Le mostré el dibujo que quería. El hombre primero miró el dibujo, y luego me miró fijamente. Suspiró profundamente, con un cansancio que parecía como si estuviera al borde de su paciencia. Al final de su suspiro, que me pareció que duró años, me invitó a pasar a otra habitación donde tenía las herramientas. Había decidido que lo quería en la parte baja de mi espalda, así que me levanté la remera y dejé que trabajara. Mientras él preparaba sus elementos, yo me sacaba fotos para compartir con mis amigos. Cuando intenté sacarle una foto al tatuador, él sólo levantó la mirada, resopló, y siguió trabajando. Me parece que no le gusté.

Finalmente terminó, y pude verme en el espejo. ¡Qué increíble que estaba mi tatuaje nuevo! ¡Encima hizo que mis gatitos tengan los ojos rojos, justo algo que hace que les resalten sus hermosas narices! Le pagué al señor, y me fui contenta del lugar. Cuando me di cuenta de que me faltó tomarme una foto con el señor, giré y me di cuenta que el local no estaba más. ¡Qué raro! Bueno, no importaba, yo tenía un tatuaje nuevo.

Al llegar a mi casa, noté que mi vecino otra vez estaba escuchando música muy fuerte. Discutí varias veces con él la última semana, y todas esas veces terminaron conmigo llorando muy frustrada. Intenté juntar fuerzas para golpearle la puerta y prepararme para discutir, pero el cansancio era mucho mayor. No pensé que tener un tatuaje iba a cansarme tanto, nadie me había dicho nada al respecto. Le di de comer a mis gatitos, y me acosté. Ni siquiera logré llegar a cambiarme, que el sueño y el cansancio me sobrepasaron. Estaba tan cansada, que ni siquiera el ruido de mi vecino fue suficiente para mantenerme despierta. Mis sueños fueron bastante raros, llenos de sombras y figuras oscuras que sentía cerca de mí, y una voz fría que me preguntaba si deseaba ayuda.

Me despertaron mis gatitos arañando asustados mi cara, y cuando abrí mis ojos, sentí una presencia en mi habitación. Al mirar el pie de mi cama, noté una figura alta, llena de huesos y vestido sólo con una túnica negra que flameaba, aunque no hubiera ningún tipo de viento. Cuando habló, note que cada fibra de mi cuerpo temblaba y tenía miedo.

¿Por qué te atreves a despertarme?

¿Yo lo desperté? – Pregunté incrédula

Así es, humana. Dime, ¿cómo lo logró un mero humano como tú?

Asustada, me levanté y me acerqué hacia la puerta de la habitación. Cuando intenté abrir la puerta, la cerradura se trabó y no importara cuánta fuerza hiciera, era imposible abrirla. Estaba encerrada en la habitación con… eso. La figura misteriosa notó mis movimientos y vislumbró mi tatuaje.

Ah, entonces ése fue el método. Esa marca que llevas en la espalda. Debí haberlo sospechado.

¿Mi tatuaje? ¿Qué tiene que ver mi tatuaje?

Soy un espíritu milenario que vivió en el comienzo de la Humanidad. Fui apresado, gracias a la magia negra, en una marca como la que tienes en la espalda. Aunque… la marca original no tenía esos animales.

¡Hey, no digas nada malo de mis gatitos!

Según mi castigo y mi maldición, debo servir y cumplir los deseos de la persona que lleve la marca.

Quedé en silencio. ¿Yo… dar órdenes? Ni siquiera puedo lograr que mis gatitos tomen su medicina.

¿Qué tipo de deseos puedes cumplir?

Los que desees. Puedo crear fuego, por ejemplo, y destruir las aldeas de tus enemigos.

Y al decir esto, levantó una mano huesuda, y en la punta de sus dedos, aparecieron pequeñas llamas de color azul.

Ah… Mira… No sé cómo decírtelo, pero… - Saqué mi encendedor de uno de los cajones de mi mesa de luz y lo encendí - La Humanidad ya tiene control sobre el fuego desde hace muchos años ya.

Huh. Era esperable. También tengo la habilidad de iluminar la cueva más profunda.

De su cara, salieron rayos de luces que lograban apenas iluminar mis sábanas. Simplemente tomé mi celular, encendí la linterna, y se la mostré.

Lo siento, señor Espíritu, pero la verdad es que no me está impresionando. Si no va a hacer nada interesante, le voy a pedir que se retire, por favor.

El espíritu, ya recurriendo a sus últimos trucos que tenía a su disposición, extendió sus brazos, o al menos, lo que parecían ser sus brazos, y en su túnica negra comenzaron a aparecer nebulosas. Cuando habló, su voz parecía más lejana y profunda.

No quería llegar a esta demostración, humana, pero no me dejas ninguna otra opción.

Pregúntame lo que desees saber, y puedo ofrecer la respuesta en cuestión de horas.

Comencé a sentirme mal por el señor Espíritu. Claramente estaba intentándolo, pero no podía dejar de notar que sus habilidades ya no eran tan importantes. Tomé de vuelta mi celular, apagué la linterna y abrí la página principal de Google. Giré el celular, y se lo mostré al señor Espíritu. Inmediatamente contrajo sus brazos, y comenzó a investigar el celular.

No entiendo. ¿Quieres decir que tienes acceso a todo el conocimiento humano habido y por haber en… este aparato?

Sí, señor Espíritu.

Entonces… ¿He sido reemplazado?

Lo siento mucho, señor Espíritu.

Largó un suspiro lleno de tristeza. Mis gatitos, como sintiendo qué es lo que le sucedía, se acercaron y comenzaron a ronronearle. Cansado y derrotado, el espíritu se sentó en el borde de la cama, y tomó la cabeza, como si estuviera contemplando la realidad de una Humanidad que ya no lo requería como antes.

¿Sabes? Guerras enteras se han librado por tener mis poderes. Reinos y civilizaciones crecieron y cayeron gracias a mis habilidades. Mi padre me había dicho que esto podía pasarme, pero no pensé que fuera tan pronto. ¡Mírame, todavía soy joven!

No quiero ser ofensiva, pero… ¿cuántos años tiene?

Sólo tengo cien mil años. ¡Todavía soy joven!

Traté de consolarlo, acariciando su espalda y diciendo que todo iba a estar bien. La realidad es que no sabía cómo lograr que se calme. No soy buena calmando a mis amigas, así que menos voy a serlo con un espíritu milenario.

Bueno, señor Espíritu, ya está… Dígame… ¿acaso no tiene alguna otra habilidad especial?

Bueno… Durante estos años, aprendí a cocinar… - Dijo entre lo que sonaban como lágrimas — pero nunca nadie me pidió que les cocine algo. Todos querían destrucción y terror a sus enemigos, ¡y yo soy mucho más que eso!

Al elevar la voz, los cuadros en mi pieza temblaron y se escuchaba que las alarmas de los autos cercanos comenzaban a sonar. Vi, finalmente, una posibilidad de ayudarlo.

¿Sabes cocinar? ¡Eso es genial!

¿En serio?

¡Sí! Yo nunca supe cómo cocinar. Siempre quemé la comida, y nunca pude seguir las más simples instrucciones. Una vez me dijeron que cocinara con sal marina, y pensé que había que ir a la playa para buscarla.

Comenzó a reír. Hasta a mis gatitos les gustó el sonido de esa risa.

Está bien, humana. Puedo cocinarte lo que quieras.

¿En serio? ¡Sí! ¡Muchas gracias, señor Espíritu!

Traté de abrazarlo, pero su forma huesuda me lastimó. Estaba muy feliz. Creo que conseguí un amigo nuevo.

Questionnaire

- Do you have a tattoo?
- Be honest: If a millennial spirit appeared in your bedroom, what would you do?
- If you have pets, do they understand you when you are having a bad or a sad day?
- What do they do to cheer you up?
- In as few sentences as possible, try to write what the day to day would be between the protagonist and the spirit. Here's a tip: what kind of food would it cook? Normal food or weird, spiritual food? In Spanish!

Let's review some grammar and fun facts!

In Spanish, we have few words to talk about small kittens: gatito, meaning "little cat" or "kitten." In English, we have several. It is one of the few instances where the opposite is true, since normally, it would happen backwards.

Obviously, there are a lot of ways to talk about kittens in a colloquial way, for example, michi, michifuz, etc.

There are no correct translations for those terms, and since they depend on the place of South America that you are reading about (or talking to someone from), it will always vary. The basic of that sound is the pronunciation of the miau sound, and that's a basis for the michi/michifuz name.

Try to tell your Spanish friends that, and you will find that it's an amazing detail that they probably didn't know!

Translation

Finally, I decided to do the dumbest thing in my life. Friends and family members said that I shouldn't do it, even my own conscience convinced me that I shouldn't. But I was decided: I got a tattoo.

Choosing it wasn't easy. At first, I thought of doing something related to my little kittens, maybe a paw or something that reminds me how much I love them. But then, when I started to see designs, I realized that a lot of people do that kind of stuff and the truth is that I didn't want to go with the flow of what other people do.

I always defined myself as a pretty singular and special girl, so the last thing that I wanted to do is to follow the crowd.

My research took me to find tribal symbols, similar to what my personal trainer at the gym had. Those I liked even more, but again, my research showed me that everybody used something like it.

Close to frustration and on the edge of letting go of my whim, I finally found what I wanted: two stars surrounding a small animal inside. I loved it! It looked so cute to me, and if I managed to change and make the tattooist to insert my kittens, it would look so much better.

After choosing the design, it came the time to find the best price for someone who had a small budget like me. Each tattooist that I visited asked me for a fortune to make it, and I couldn't understand why. After all, it's just a couple of lines, a bit of drawing, color, shadow, also to adapt the faces of my babies to the tattoo, and, of course, doing it quick and perfect. It couldn't cost that much.

Luckily, I found a tattooist. In an abandoned neighborhood, close to a cemetery, one day that rained a lot, and I only realized because thunder lightened up the sign that said that there was a tattooist who charged cheap for his work. What a coincidence! When I went in, the tattooist stared at me. He had a long beard and a penetrating gaze. He looked me up and down, and asked me if I wanted a tattoo.

"How did you know that?"

"Because I'm a tattooist. People don't come in here searching for information on the soccer matches."

"Ah, right, I replied. "Can you tattoo me this little drawing, but with some kittens?"

I showed him the drawing that I wanted. The man first looked at the drawing, and then stared at me. He sighed deeply, with an exhaustion that looked like it was on the edge of his patience. At the end of his sigh, which seemed to me that lasted years, he invited me to go to the next room where he had his tools. I had decided that I wanted it on the lower part of my back so I lifted up my shirt and let him work. While he prepared his instruments, I took photos to share with my friends. When I tried to take a picture of the tattooist, he only looked up, snorted, and continued to work. I think he didn't like me.

He finally finished, and I could look myself in the mirror. How amazing it looked, my new tattoo!

And he managed to make my kittens have red eyes, exactly what highlights their beautiful noses! I paid the man, and I happily left the place.

When I realized that I forgot to take a picture with him, I turned and realized that the place wasn't there any more. That's weird! Oh well, it didn't matter, I had a new tattoo.

When I arrived home, I realized that my neighbor was again listening to music really loud. I argued with him several times last week, and all those times ended up with me crying really frustrated.

I tried to gather strength to knock on his door and prepared to argue, but the exhaustion was far worse. I didn't think that having a tattoo was going to tire me so much, no one had ever said to me anything like that.

I fed my kittens, and I went to bed. I didn't even manage to change my clothes, sleep and tiredness overwhelmed me. I was so tired, that not even my neighbor's noise was enough to keep me awake. My dreams were really weird, full of shadows and dark shapes that I felt close to me, and a cold voice asked me if I needed help.

My kittens woke me up by scratching my face, and when I opened my eyes, I felt a presence in my room. When I looked at the foot of my bed, there was a tall figure, full of bones and dressed up in a flaring black tunic, even if there weren't any kind of wind. When he spoke, I noticed that every fiber of my body shook and was afraid.

"Why do you dare to wake me up?"

"Did I wake you up?"I asked incredulously.

"That's right, human. Tell me how a human like you managed to do it."

Scared, I got up and got close to the door of my bedroom. When I tried to open the door, the lock got stuck and no matter how much force I used, it was impossible to open it. I was locked up inside my bedroom with… that. The mysterious figure noticed my movements and saw my tattoo.

"Ah, so that was the method. That mark you carry on your back. I should have guessed."

"My tattoo? What my tattoo has to do with you?"

"I am a millennial spirit that lived since the beginning of Humankind. I was jailed, thanks to black magic, in a mark like the one you have on your back. Although… the original mark didn't have those animals."

"Hey, don't say anything about my kittens!"

"According to my punishment and my curse, I must obey and fulfill the wishes of the person who has the mark."

I was silent. Me… giving orders? I can't even make my kittens take their medicine.

"What kind of wishes can you make?"

"Whatever you want. I can create fire, for example, and destroy the villages of your enemies."

And saying this, he showed a bony hand and, at the tips of his fingers, appeared small blue flames.

"Ah… Look… I don't know how to say it, but…" I took out my lighter from one drawer of my night table and lighted up. "Humankind already has control over fire for a lot of years now."

"Huh. It was to be expected. I also have the ability to illuminate the deepest cave."

From its face, there were rays of light that barely were able to illuminate my sheets. I simply took out my cell phone, turned on the light, and showed it to him.

"I'm sorry, Mr Spirit, but the truth is that you are not impressing me. If you are not going to do something interesting, I'm going to ask you to leave, please."

The spirit, already using his last tricks in his sleeve, extended his arms, or at least, what looked like his arms, and in his black tunic, nebulae started to appear. When he spoke, his voice appeared far away and deep.

"I didn't want to reach this demonstration, human, but you leave me no choice. Ask me anything you wish to know, and I can offer you the answer in a matter of hours."

I started to feel bad for Mr Spirit. It was clearly trying, but I couldn't stop noticing that his skills weren't that important anymore. I took my cell phone again, turned off the flashlight, and opened the Google homepage. I turned the cell phone, and showed it to Mr Spirit. It immediately contracted its arms and started to investigate the cell phone.

"I don't understand. Are you trying to say that you have access to the entire human knowledge in this… device?"

"Yes, Mr Spirit."

"So… I have been replaced?"

"I'm so sorry, Mr Spirit."

He sighed full of sadness. My kittens, feeling what was happening with him, went closer and started to purr. Tired and defeated, the spirit sat on the edge of the bed and shook his head, like he was contemplating the reality of a Humankind that he didn't know that much anymore.

"Do you know? Entire wars took place to get my powers. Kingdoms and civilizations grew and fell thanks to my abilities. My father told me this might happen to me, but I didn't think that it would happen so soon. Look at me, I'm still young!"

"I don't want to be rude, but… how old are you?"

"I'm only a thousand years old. I'm still young!"

I tried to comfort him, rubbing his back and telling him that everything was going to be alright. The reality is that I didn't know how to calm him down. I'm not good at comforting my friends, and I would be even worse with a millennial spirit.

"Well, Mr Spirit, it's okay… Tell me… don't you have any other special skill?"

"Well… during all these years, I learned to cook…"He replied between what sounded like tears. "But no one has ever asked me to cook something. They all wanted destruction and terror to their enemies, and I'm much more than that!"

When he raised his voice, the pictures in my bedroom shook and you could listen to the alarms of the closest cars that started to sound. I saw, finally, a way to help him.

"Do you know how to cook? That's great!"

"Really?"

"Yeah! I never knew how to cook. I always burned the food, and I never could follow the simplest instruction. Once they told me that I had to cook with sea salt, and I thought that I had to go to the beach to get it."

The spirit started to laugh. Even my kittens liked the sound of that laugh.

"All right, human. I can cook anything you want."

"Really? Yeah! Thank you so much, Mr Spirit!"

I tried to hug him but his bony shape hurt me. I was so happy. I think I found a new friend.

"FALTA DE MODALES A LA HORA DE VESTIR/LACK OF MANNERS WHEN IT COMES TO DRESSING"

Para serles honesto, yo no creía en los fantasmas. Cada vez que leía una historia de hechos sobrenaturales, pensaba en que la gente era fácil de engañar, o que confundía hechos con ficción. E incluso, lograba encontrarle una explicación lógica a lo que la gente creía que eran fantasmas o espíritus. Cada vez que leía que había una casa encantada donde los cuadros temblaban, yo pensaba que posiblemente el viento a través de alguna rendija los hacía mover, o que en las cercanías había alguna autopista que generaba ese temblor. Por cada historia de poltergeists, o espíritus demoníacos, yo tenía una respuesta ideal.

Por eso, comencé a escribir varios artículos sobre mis ideas en el periódico local. Esto me dio fama de escéptico, y fui invitado a dar charlas a lo largo de todo el país. La gente solía enfrentarme con sus historias de posesiones, o invitarme a sus hogares donde juraban que en la habitación había fantasmas o que el espíritu de su perrito muerto los visitaba todas las noches. Y ante cada una de estas invitaciones, siempre les daba la respuesta racional e inteligente, y siempre se ofendían conmigo. Me decían que no creía en nada, y que para poder ver los seres del más allá uno tenía que creer en algo.

Por eso, cuando me invitaron al hogar de los Perez, no pensé que iba a ser distinto a lo que ya había experimentado antes. Me habían dejado una nota, y enviado las llaves por correo. En la nota, me daban rienda libre para poder revisar el hogar sin ningún de restricción, y que podía quedarme el tiempo que quisiera. Si decidía irme, sólo tenía que avisar al vecino, que él estaría en contacto con ellos para darles la llave. Empaqué un poco de ropa, y un diario para poder escribir todo lo que encontraba.

Llegué al hogar de los Perez, y la verdad es que de fuera no me parecía muy tétrica. Sí, lucía un poco descuidada, pero nada que un poco de pintura y cuidado no pudieran solucionar. Me elegí una de las habitaciones, y desempaqué. La primera noche no fue muy llamativa, y sólo porque el viento por momentos no me dejó dormir, podría decir que fue una noche muy tranquila. Cuando me desperté al día siguiente, noté que mis camisas y remeras estaban desordenadas, pero eso se podía explicar porque al llegar el día anterior, las había ordenado de cualquier manera Pero, al tratar de ordenarlas, noté que están pegadas a la maleta. Atrás mío, sentí una pequeña risa. Giré y lo vi: Un ser transparente que miraba con una sonrisa burlona.

      ¿De verdad creías que podías combinar una camisa blanca abierta con una remera de rock pesado? ¿Acaso no te enseñaron nada?

Quedé en silencio. Los Perez no me habían dicho nada sobre qué tipo de fantasma era, simplemente que era muy molesto. La figura me miraba, y esperaba una respuesta. A pesar de mis anteriores experiencias, nunca había visto un fantasma en la vida real. De hecho, todavía seguía sin creerlo.

¿Quién eres? – Pregunté con un tono incrédulo.

¿Ahora? Un fantasma ¿Antes? Diseñador de vestuario. Pero eso no contesta mi pregunta. ¿Acaso no te enseñaron nada de cómo vestirte?

Mira, creo que no tenemos la confianza suficiente como para que me juzgues de esa manera.

Yo voy a juzgar a cualquier persona que se atreva a combinar la ropa de la manera tan horrible que lo hiciste tú.

Pero eres un fantasma, no puedes darme consejos de vestuario.

No sólo no combinas los colores y las texturas de un modo correcto, sino que, además, no escuchas. Yo era diseñador ¡Diseñador! Yo trabajaba haciendo esto. Los grandes actores de Hollywood requerían mis servicios. Scarlett Johanson, George Clooney, Chris Pratt, Ryan Gosling, Emma Stone

El fantasma continuó enumerando actores famosos a los que les diseñó. Los premios que recibió. Las películas en las trabajó. Y yo no podía dejar de pensar que era demasiado insoportable. Siguió con su discurso durante al menos 5 minutos, y yo estaba seguro que estaba mintiendo.

Mira, señor… señor Fantasma, me convocaron aquí porque me pidieron que investigue si usted era un fantasma de verdad o si había alguna otra respuesta.

¿Entonces?

Bueno, puedo llegar a una sola conclusión: Usted es un fantasma.

Wow, increíble. De verdad eres muy inteligente.

Su tono sarcástico no ayuda a la situación…

Está bien, está bien. Me quedo en silencio.

Gracias. Como decía, usted es un fantasma. Pero no un fantasma cualquiera. Usted es un fantasma insoportable.

La mirada de desilusión del fantasma, debo decir, me partió el corazón.

Oiga, oiga, tranquilo señor. Puedo ofrecerle algo, fantasma.

Lo escucho – Contestó triste el fantasma.

Usted deje en paz a los Perez, yo les daré alguna explicación que los deje contentos, y usted viene conmigo.

Pero… ¿por qué me ofrece eso?

Bueno, usted mismo lo dijo, señor fantasma: Porque no sé vestirme.

Como les decía, yo no creía en los fantasmas. Hasta hace un año. Ahora, si me disculpan, tengo que retirarme. Me invitaron a una fiesta de premiación al mejor vestido del año.

QUESTIONNAIRE

- Do you believe in ghosts or paranormal activities?
- Have you ever seen a ghost? What about a haunted house?
- The ghost in the story is still a costume designer in the afterlife. If that happened to you, what would you be? What kind of profession would you have?
- And if you could switch professions, what would you choose?

Let's review some grammar and fun facts!

In South America, there are a lot of stories about ghosts. One of the most famous is the chupacabra, which isn't exactly a ghost, but no one can actually tell you what it is. Some say it is an animal, others say that it is a spirit, and some people say that it is an experiment made by the government.

Try to compare the supernatural stories from your country or city, to the kind of stories in South America. You will find that they have an amazing tradition on ghosts, possessions and poltergeists.

TRANSLATION

To be honest, I didn't believe in ghosts. Every time I read a story of supernatural cases, I thought people were easy to deceive, or they confused facts with fiction.

I manage to find a logical explanation for what people believed were ghost or spirits. Every time I read that there was a haunted house where the pictures shook, I thought that maybe the wind through a crack made them move, or that nearby there was some highway that generated that shake. For each story of poltergeist, or demonic spirits, I had a perfect answer.

Because of that, I started to write several articles about my ideas in the local newspaper. This gave me certain fame as a skeptic and was invited to lecture all over the country.

People used to confront me with their stories of possessions or invite me to their homes where they swore the room had ghosts or that the spirit of their dead dog visited them every night. And to each of those invitations, I always gave them the rational and smart answer, and they always got angry with me. They said that I didn't believe in anything, and to be able to see the afterlife beings you have to believe in something.

That's why, when I was invited to the Perez home, I didn't think it was going to be any different to what I had already experienced.

I had received a note and got the keys by mail. In the note, they gave me free rein to check out the home without any kind of restriction, and I could stay as long as I wished. If I decided to go, I only had to let the neighbor know, and he would be in contact with them to give them the key back. I packed up some clothes, and a diary to write anything that might happen.

I arrived at the Perez home, and the reality is that from the outside it didn't look very scary. Yes, it was a bit ruined, but nothing that a bit of painting and care couldn't fix. I chose one of the bedrooms and unpacked. The first night wasn't very eventful, and apart from wind that didn't let me sleep, I could say that it was a very quiet night.

When I woke up the next day, I noticed that my shirts and t-shirts were messy, but that could be explained because when I arrived the day before, I sorted them out randomly. But, when I tried to tidy them, I noticed that they were stuck to the suitcase. Behind me, I heard a small laugh. I turned and saw it: A transparent being that looked on with a smile on its face.

> "Did you really think that you could combine a white shirt with a heavy metal t-shirt? Haven't they thought you anything?"

I fell into silence. The Perezes hadn't said anything about what kind of ghost it was, just that it was really annoying. The shape looked at me and hoped for an answer. Despite all my previous experiences, I had never seen a ghost in real life. In fact, I still couldn't believe it.

> "Who are you?" I asked with a skeptical tone.

> "Now? A ghost. Before? Costume designer. But that doesn't answer my question. Haven't they thought you anything about how to dress?"

> "Look, I think we don't know each other well enough for you to judge me that way."

> "I'm going to judge anybody who dares to combine clothes the horrible way you do."

> "But you are a ghost, you can't give me clothing advice."

> "You don't only just combine colors and textures in a bad way, but you also don't listen. I was a designer. Designer! I worked doing this. Hollywood's biggest actors required my services. Scarlett Johansson, George Clooney, Chris Pratt, Ryan Gosling, Emma Stone…"

The ghost continued naming famous actors which he had designed for. The awards he received. The movies he worked on. And I couldn't stop thinking that it was too intolerable. It went on with its speech for at least five more minutes, and I was sure that he was lying.

> "Look, mister… mister Ghost, I was invited here because they asked me to investigate if you were a real ghost or if there were any other answers."

> "So?"

> "Well, I can reach one conclusion: You are a ghost."

"Wow, incredible. You really are smart."

"Your sarcastic tone isn't helping the situation…"

"All right, all right. I will stay quiet."

"Thank you. Like I was saying, you are a ghost. But not just any ghost. You are an insufferable ghost."

The look of disappointment, I have to say, broke my heart.

"Hey, hey, easy sir. I can offer you something, ghost."

"I'm listening,"sadly replied the ghost.

"You leave the Perezes alone, I give them some explanation that makes them happy, and you are coming with me."

"But… why are you offering me this?"

"Well, you said it yourself, mister ghost: Because I don't know how to dress."

Like I was saying, I didn't believe in ghosts. Until a year ago. Now, if you excuse me, I have to go. I was invited to a celebration to the best dressed of the year.

"LOS VIEJOS, EL ÁRBOL Y EL CAFÉ/THE OLD MEN, THE TREE AND THE COFFEE PLACE"

En el viejo café del barrio, cerca de un antiguo árbol, se solían reunir dos señores de edad mayor. En ese café, trabajé durante todo un verano, tratando de conseguir algunos pesos y poder tomarme unas vacaciones.

La mesa que siempre elegía esa inusual pareja era la mesa que se encontraba justo al lado de la ventana, a donde daba la sombra del árbol. Uno de los dos era ciego, y el otro tenía problemas para caminar, y utilizaba unos bastones. Siempre pedían café con leche, y un vaso de agua. Sus conversaciones parecían muy interesantes, porque siempre se los veía animados, sonriendo, y gesticulando con los brazos.

Un día, me tocó llevarles su pedido. Por alguna razón, quizás un rumor o porque lo había leído en algún periódico, yo estaba seguro que eran escritores. No lo había confirmado, pero mientras le servía el café y el vaso de agua, se los pregunté.

Disculpen, ¿ustedes son escritores?

El hombre ciego giró su cabeza hacia mí, y me contestó.

No, nene, somos jugadores de fútbol, y todos los domingos jugamos en el equipo del barrio. Él patea – señalando a su amigo – y yo atajo.

El silencio incómodo inundó el ambiente, hasta que el hombre ciego sonrió y largó la más sonora carcajada que jamás escuché. Una carcajada viva, llena de juventud y alegría. Me retiré de la mesa un poco más tranquilo sabiendo que no los había ofendido.

Al poco tiempo, el ayuntamiento decidió cortar el árbol, ya que consideraban que era muy viejo y que podía caerse en cualquier momento. Llegaron con sus máquinas y lo derribaron. Fue un día muy triste en el barrio. Luego de eso, nunca más volvieron a aparecer el señor ciego y su amigo. Siempre me quedará la duda de si eran escritores o no.

QUESTIONNAIRE

- Do you have any special places to take coffee or eat? What is it like?
- What do you think happened to the odd couple in the story? Do you think they are still alive?
- What do you think the odd couple were? Writers?
- Rewrite the ending to make it a happy ending. Here's a hint: What about the main character? Maybe he searched for them.

Let's review some grammar and fun facts!

Did you know that the characters are based on Ernesto Sábato and Jorge Luis Borges? They were incredible writers, and if you have the opportunity, you should try to read some of their works, which might be a bit hard to understand if you started learning the language, but believe me, they are worth it. They used to have coffee in a small coffee place in San Telmo, Buenos Aires, Argentina.

On the grammar side of this story, we find the usual conundrum between football or soccer. In Spanish, football means the usual sport that we all know, and the NFL and its sports is called American Football, in order to distinguish it from the usual (and far more entertaining, if you ask me!) sports that South American love.

TRANSLATION

In the old coffee place of the neighborhood, close to an old tree, two old people used to gather. In that coffee shop, I worked for an entire summer, trying to earn some pesos and go on vacations.

The table that the unusual couple always chose was the table right next to the window, where the shadow of the tree was. One of them was blind, and the other had walking problems and used a special cane. They always asked for coffee with milk and a glass of water. Their conversations seemed very interesting, because they always looked lively, smiling and gesticulating with their arms.

One day, I had to take them their order. For some reason, maybe a rumor or because I had read it in some newspaper, I was sure that they were writers. I hadn't confirmed it, but while I was serving them their coffee and the glass of water, I asked them:

"Excuse me, are you writers?"

The blind man turned his head to me and replied.

"No, kiddo, we are football players, and every Sunday we play in the neighborhood
team. He kicks" – pointing at his friend – "and I'm a goalkeeper.

The uncomfortable silence flooded the place until the blind man smiled and had the loudest
laugh that I've ever heard. A lively laugh, full of youth and joy. I left the table a bit more calm
knowing that I hadn't offended them.

Soon after this, the city council decided to cut down the tree, because they considered that it
was too old and it might fall at any time. They arrived with their machines and cut it down. It
was a really sad day in the neighborhood. After that, the blind man and his friend never
showed up again. I will always have doubt if they were writers or not.

"Crimen/Crime"

Juan tomó su arma, se levantó de su silla, y salió. Subió a su auto de policía, encendió la radio, y comenzó a patrullar el barrio. Era un barrio bastante tranquilo, donde prácticamente nada sucedía, más allá de algún pequeño robo de bicicletas, o algún altercado entre los niños del colegio secundario que se encontraba a unas pocas cuadras de la estación de policía.

Patrulló durante todo el día. Llegó a su casa, besó a su mujer, y a su hija, cenaron los tres juntos, se duchó y luego se acostaron a ver un poco de televisión antes de dormir. En las noticias, escuchó sobre el enorme aumento del crimen en todo el país. Eso le pareció raro a Juan, quien jamás vio un crimen mayor que alguna discusión familiar.

Al día siguiente, hizo su rutina de todos los días, pero al patrullar comenzó a mirar todo a su alrededor con aire extrañado. ¿Será verdad lo que dicen las noticias todos los días? ¿Era cierto que había caos, y destrucción en cada una de las ciudades de la Tierra? No, no podía ser.

Al llegar al borde del pueblo, subió a una pequeña colina, y se tomó unos minutos para contemplar la ciudad. Quizás estaban equivocados. El crimen estaba allá lejos, fuera de la ciudad, y aquí dentro estaban seguros. Sí, lo más probable era que nunca iba a suceder ahí. No mientras esté Juan. Además, más allá de los problemas menores que a veces pueden suceder, ¿qué tipo de crimen podía pasar en el Paraíso?

QUESTIONNAIRE

- What do you think it happened to Juan?
- Do you believe in Paradise?
- What kind of Paradise do you believe in?
- Write down your version of Paradise, but here's a catch: You have to make it in five sentences or less.

Let's review some grammar and fun facts!

The paradise in Spanish is mostly associated with open fields and green pastures, and not a city. But if you go to some parts of Perú, they will tell you the other way around.

Like we did before, we found names that we cannot translate. If you ever meet a Spanish person, ask him if he or she wants his/her name translated when in a normal conversation. Some people are okay with it, but some people don't like it.

TRANSLATION

Juan took his gun, got up his chair, and got out. Got inside his police car, turned on the radio, and started to patrol the neighborhood. It was a really quiet neighborhood, where practically nothing happened, beyond some small bike theft, or some altercation between the kids of the high school that were a few blocks from the police station.

He patrolled all day. Came home, kissed his wife, and his daughter, had dinner with them, had a shower and then they lay down to watch some television before sleeping. In the news, he heard about the huge increase in crime all over the country. That looked weird to Juan, who had never seen a worse crime than a family argument.

The next day, he did his everyday routine, but when he was patrolling he started to look everywhere with a bewildered look. Was it true what the news said every day? Was it true that there were chaos and destruction in each city on Earth? No, it couldn't be.

When he reached the edge of the town, he went up to a small hill and took a few minutes to contemplate the city. Maybe they were wrong. The crime was far away, out of the city, and here they were safe. Yeah, most likely that it wasn't going to happen there. Not while Juan was there. Besides, leaving aside the small problems that might happen, what kind of crime might happen in Paradise?

"Horrible manera de despertar/Horrible way to wake up"

El jueves fue un día normal para Esteban. Se levantó, se vistió, asistió a clases, luego almorzó, llegó a casa, se puso a estudiar, luego descansó un poco jugando con la Playstation, Luego cenó con sus padres, se duchó y se acostó para dormir. Un día normal como todos.

Se despertó el día viernes, pero ya de inmediato notó algo raro. No parecía que estaba en su propia habitación. Los posters y las fotos no eran las de él, ni tampoco parecía el mismo diseño de habitación. De hecho, parecía una casa completamente distinta. Trató de vestirse, pero también notó que sus ropas eran distintas, de un tamaño mucho mayor al que normalmente usaba. Al llegar al baño, pudo mirarse al espejo. Esteban, quien era joven y vital, tenía un aspecto demacrado, viejo, como si hubiera dormido durante los últimos sesenta años. Sus manos parecían gastadas, ya arruinadas con el paso del tiempo. No tenía ya dientes, y su pelo era bastante escaso.

Trató de buscar ayuda, donde fuera posible encontrarla. Recorrió la casa rápidamente, o al menos, lo más rápido que sus frágiles huesos le permitieron. Al llegar al borde de una escalera, tropezó y cayó. El dolor lo hizo despertarse.

Esteban abrió los ojos asustado, y revisó su habitación. Todo estaba en orden. ¿Qué era lo que había pasado? Corriendo, fue hacia el baño. Era él, no un señor viejo y feo. Respiró con tranquilidad. Ya había pasado, había sido todo una pesadilla.

Questionnaire

- What happened to Esteban?
- Who do you think is the old man?
- Have you ever had a dream that you swore it could have been real?
- Let's say that you woke up and you think you are not in your body: What would you do? What are the first things you would do to see if you are in your body or to find out what happened?

Let's review some grammar and fun facts!

One of the fun things about Spanish is that people use "old man" not as an insult, but as a sign of respect. But not all people like it, so be careful when approaching the subject in a conversation.

For example, one of my closest friend's father hates the term, because it makes him feel useless. So before going out saying "viejo" to everyone you meet, try to understand the other person you are talking to, and see if he will find it very disrespectful or not.

Translation

Thursday was a normal day for Esteban. He got up, got dressed, went to classes, then had lunch, came home, studied, then he rested for a while playing with the PlayStation. After that, he had dinner with his parents, had a shower and laid down to sleep. A normal day like any.

He woke up on Friday, but immediately he noticed something strange. It didn't look like he was in his own room.

The posters and pictures weren't what he had, nor did it look like the same room design. In fact, it looked like a completely different house.

He tried to get dressed, but he also noticed that his clothes were different, of a size much larger than what he normally used. When he reached the bathroom, he could take a look in the mirror. Esteban, who was young and vital, had a gaunt look, old, like if he had slept during the past sixty years. His hands looked worn out, already ruined by the passage of time. He didn't have any teeth left, and his hair was pretty scarce.

He tried to get help, where it was possible to find it. He searched the house quickly, or at least, as quickly as his old fragile bones allowed him. When he reached the end of the stairs, he tripped and fell. The pain made him woke up.

Esteban opened his eyes scared, and check out his bedroom. Everything was in order. What had happened? Running, he went to the bathroom. It was him, not an old and ugly man. He calmly breathes. It already passed, it was just a nightmare.

"Viaje Intergaláctico/Intergalactic travel"

Tatiana abrió los ojos, respiró profundamente, y trató de distinguir su habitación. El viaje había sido bastante extraño, un poco doloroso, pero al menos fue casi instantáneo. Se encontraba en un momento en un lugar de la galaxia, y luego, en el otro. No recordaba exactamente porqué estaba acá, pero sabía que tenía un objetivo.

Al explorar a su alrededor notó que tenía solamente dos piernas, y solamente dos manos. Era raro, porque le habían prometido que iba a tener más. Pero pensó que quizás era un error de su memoria. Al levantarse, admiró con qué facilidad su cuerpo se adaptó a la gravedad de ese planeta. Probó sus piernas. Primero dobló una rodilla, luego la otra. Con qué facilidad lo hacían aquí. Pensar que estaba acostubrada a no tener rodillas o huesos en absoluto en su galaxia. Bajó hacia el piso inferior del hogar, y decidió ingerir algunos alimentos. Cuando abrió la heladera, vio una pequeña caja de cartón de color blanco con unas letras que decían "LECHE". Eso le recordó algo. Quizás era su propósito. Quizás tenía que ver con su objetivo en la Tierra.

Tomó la caja, y vertió su líquido en el interior de un recipiente de vidrio. Cuando la probó, sus papilas gustativas se activaron con miles de sensaciones distintas. Con que esto era el sabor. Podía comprender por qué los humanos se volvían desesperados por conseguir más y más variaciones de sabores, llegando a mezclar cualquier cosa que se pudiera comer.

Salió del hogar, aun completamente sobrepasada por la mera idea de que existieran tantos sabores en algo tan simple como un líquido blanco, cuando una figura familiar la detuvo.

KVUY89, tienes que volver – dijo esa figura con forma de sombra – Nos equivocamos.

¿A qué te refieres? – Contestó Tatiana asustada

Sí, teníamos que enviarte para que investigues el planeta desde la forma de una vaca, y… bueno, nos equivocamos. Culpo al retraso de la transmisión intergaláctica.

Pero… pero…

Lo siento mucho. De verdad lo siento – Levantó lo que parecían ser sus dedos, e hizo un chasquido.

Tatiana despertó. Se encontraba en un establo con otros animales como ella. Entró un humano con un balde de metal y comenzó a ordeñar a uno de esos animales. No recordaba nada de su breve vida anterior.

QUESTIONNAIRE

- Do you believe in extraterrestrial beings?
- If you do, what are they like, according to you?
- Let's say one of those beings appeared in front of you today, what would happen? How would you react?
- Assuming we get intergalactic travel, where would you want to live, and why? What kind of planet would you choose?
- Write down the kind of planets you would love to visit.

Let's review some grammar and fun facts!

Here is a handy list with the names of the planets in the Solar System and their Spanish translations, just in case you ever want to visit other worlds

Sun – Sol

Mercury – Mercurio

Venus – Venus

Earth – Tierra

Mars – Marte

Jupiter – Júpiter

Saturn – Saturno

Urano – Urano

Neptune – Neptuno

Pluto – Plutón

Yes, I know Pluto isn't a planet anymore, but old habits die hard.

TRANSLATION

Tatiana opened her eyes, took a deep breath, and tried to identify her bedroom. The trip had been really strange, a bit painful, but at least it was almost instantaneous. She was on one side of the galaxy and the next one, in the other. She didn't exactly remember why she was here, but she knew she had an objective.

When she explored her surroundings, she noticed that she only had two legs, and just two hands. It was weird because she had been promised that she would have more. But she thought that maybe it was a mistake of her memory.

When she got up, she admired the ease that her body adapted to the gravity of this planet. She tried her legs. First, she bent one knee, then the other one. How easily they do it here. To think that she was used to not having knees or bones in her galaxy. She went down to the lower floor of the home and decided to ingest some food. When she opened the fridge, she saw a small white carton box with some letters that said "MILK." That reminded her of something. Maybe it was her purpose. Maybe it had to do with her objective on Earth.

She left the house, still completely overwhelmed by the mere idea that there existed so many tastes in something as simple as a white liquid when a familiar figure stopped her.

> "KVUY89, you have to go back," said that figure in the shape of a shadow. "We had a mistake."
>
> "What do you mean?" Tatiana replied, scared.
>
> "Yeah, we meant to send you to research the planet from the shape of a cow, and… well… we had a mistake. I blame the delay of the intergalactic transmission."
>
> "But… but…"
>
> "I'm so sorry. I really am." He raised what appeared to be his fingers, and snapped them.

Tatiana woke up. She found herself in a stable with other animals like her. A human with a metal bucket started to milk one of those animals. She didn't remember anything about her previous life.

"Alguien me ve/Someone's watching me"

Papá siempre nos contaba que se sentía perseguido. Desde que Mamá falleció hace cinco años, Papá no salía de casa. Sin sus anteojos, ya rotos hace años, y con su firme negación a operarse de los ojos, vivía encerrado, viendo televisión y escuchando la radio. Estaba seguro que alguien lo miraba por la ventana todos los días a la misma hora. Siempre se acercaba a la ventana del comedor, y, aunque su visión era muy borrosa debido a la edad, siempre podía distinguir una figura que lo miraba con curiosidad. Todos los días, a las cuatro de la tarde, esa misma figura lo veía sin falta.

Papá ya falleció hace una semana, y me tocaba a mí ir a su casa a buscar sus pertenencias. Entré, y de inmediato el aroma a encierro me embargó. Tantos recuerdos y tantas memorias de este hogar, y Papá ya no estaba para compartirlas con nadie. Mi hijo me ayudó a limpiar la casa. Entre tanto trabajo, olvidé qué hora era. Sonó la alarma del gran reloj del comedor indicando que eran las cuatro de la tarde, la hora en la que Papá decía que alguien lo miraba y lo espiaba.

Juan, ¿puedes ir al comedor a apagar la alarma?

Sí, papá.

Ah, y mientras estás ahí, ¿puedes fijarte si ves alguien por la ventana?

Acá no hay una ventana, hay solamente un espejo.

Questionnaire

- Do you have any glasses? (If not, you are lucky. I can't read without mine!)
- Let's assume that you find someone looking at you through a window (like the character in the story) every day at the same time. What would you do?
- Do you have big clocks in your house?
- Do you live in a big house?
- Write down, in ten sentences or less, the kind of house the old man lives in. Does it have any pictures? What about books or plants?

Let's review some grammar and fun facts!

The word "glass" is another one of those English words with three different translations: Vaso, as in glass of water, anteojos for spectacles ("I need glasses to read a book"), and vidrio, as in a glass window ("Here's my glass window"). Be mindful of the context, and like everything, practice will make you perfect.

Translation

Dad always told us that he felt persecuted. Since Mom passed away five years ago, Dad didn't get out of the house. Without his glasses, broken years ago, and with his firm denial to get eye surgery, he lived enclosed, watching television and listening to the radio. He was sure that someone watched through the windows every day at the same time.

He always got close to the dining room window, and, even though his vision was very blurry because of his age, he could always make out a shape that looked at him with curiosity. Every day, at four in the afternoon, the same shape looked at him without fail.

Dad passed away a week ago, and I had to go to his house to search for his belongings. I went in, and immediately the aroma of confinement closed up on me.

So many memories and so many recollections of this home, and Dad wasn't around to share them with anyone. My son helped me to clean up the house. Between that much work, I forgot what time it was. The alarm of the big clock in the dining room went off, indicating that it was four in the afternoon, the hour in which Dad said that someone looked and spying on him.

"Juan, can you turn off the alarm?"

"Yes, Dad."

"Ah, and while you are there, can you check out the window to see if you see someone?"

"There's no window in here, only a mirror."

"Clases de Ballet/Ballet classes"

Siempre fuimos una familia muy conservadora. Nos criamos con una institutriz llamada Susana, una señora de mucha edad, que insistía que en la familia se estudiara ballet. Decía que era bueno para la personalidad, y que formaba carácter y femineidad. Así que le hicimos caso, y todas las mujeres de la familia estudiaron ballet. Mi abuela, mi madre, y mis hermanas, todas bailaron ballet, y todas ganaron premios internacionales.

Mis hijas, por supuesto, no iban a ser la excepción. Cuando nacieron, Susana las tomó en sus brazos ya viejos, y dijo que serían increíbles bailarinas, que tenían todo el potencial de ser estrellas del ballet. Pero Susana, al poco tiempo, falleció. No podíamos estar sin institutriz, porque tanto mi esposa como yo trabajamos todo el día, así que conseguimos a María, una joven que contaba con excelentes referencias de parte de la agencia de institutrices. Ella era una joven firme pero jovial, y nuestras hijas la amaron enseguida.

Al poco tiempo de que Susana falleciera, las niñas quisieron dejar de ir a las clases de ballet. Decían que no tenía sentido, que ya nadie bailaba eso, y que preferían bailar reggaetón. No, les dijimos varias veces, tenían que continuar con la tradición familiar. Tenían que continuar con el legado de Susana, en honor a todo lo que hizo por nuestra familia. Las niñas se enojaron y protestaron, pero siguieron asistiendo a las clases de Ballet.

Un día nos llamó por teléfono la profesora de las clases de Ballet, quien nos informó que las niñas no ponían atención a las clases, y que perdían el tiempo tratando de bailar otras cosas. Había decidido que era suficiente, que iba a tener una charla seria con las niñas, y que iban a acabar con ese sueño ridículo de no continuar con el mandato familiar.

Llegué a casa temprano del trabajo, y escuché en la habitación de ellas una música muy particular, como si fuera algo tribal o quizás música de baile. Me acerqué sin hacer ningún tipo de ruido, despacio para no llamar la atención sobre mi persona. Cuando abrí la puerta, vi a María bailar reggaetón junto a las chicas. Se las veía muy felices, sin la firmeza y exigencia del ballet. Las veía libres, contentas, alegres como pocas veces había visto en mi vida. Quizás estaba equivocado.

Esa noche tuve una conversación con mi esposa. Que estudien lo que quieran. Que no estén atrapadas en su vida por mandatos de gente que era de otra época.

Que sean felices.

QUESTIONNAIRE

- What was the kind of dance the girls hated?
- And what about the kind they loved?
- Have you ever met a governess?

Let's review some grammar and fun facts!

In South America, it's very normal to have chaperones, but not governesses. And reggaetón is a really popular type of music in South America and parts of Europe. A couple of artists are Pitbull or Wisin and Yandel.

One of my suggestions about learning a new language is to listen to some music on the language that you want to learn. Reggaetón is a good way to do it, while you also dance!

TRANSLATION

We were always a conservative family. We grew up with a governess named Susana, a lady of old age, who insisted that in the family we had to study ballet. She said that it was good for identity and that it shaped character and femininity. So we listened to her, and all the women in the family studied ballet. My grandmother, my mother, and my sisters, they all studied ballet, and they all won international awards.

My daughters, of course, wouldn't be the exception. When they were born, Susana took them on her already old arms and said that they were going to be excellent dancers, that they had all the potential to be ballet stars. But Susana, soon after that, passed away. We couldn't be without a governess, because both my wife and I work all day long, so we hired María, a young lady who had excellent references from the governess agency. She was a young firm but cheerful, and our daughters loved her right away.

Soon after Susana passed away, the girls wanted to stop going to the ballet classes. They said that it didn't make sense, that no one danced that anymore, and that they preferred to dance reggaeton. No, we said several times, they had to continue with the family tradition. They had to continue with Susana's legacy, in honor of all she did for our family. The girls got angry and protested, but they continued to assist the ballet classes.

One day the ballet teacher called us over the phone, and told us that the girls didn't care for the classes and that they wasted their time trying to dance some other dance. I decided that it was enough, that I would have a serious talk with the girls, and that they will have to stop with that ridiculous dream of not continuing the family tradition.

I came home early from work, and I heard from their room a very particular music like it was something tribal or maybe dance music. I got closer without making any kind of noise, slowly so I wouldn't attract attention to myself. When I opened the door, I saw María dancing reggaeton with the girls. They looked so happy, without the firmness and demand of the ballet. I saw them free, happy, full of joy like few times I had seen them in my life. Maybe I was wrong.

That night I had a conversation with my wife. Let them study whatever they want. They shouldn't be trapped in their lives because of other people's mandates that are from another time.

Let them be happy.

"La casa llena de moscas/The house full of flies"

Mi casa está llena de mosquitos. No importa a qué hora del día ni qué época del año se trate, siempre hay mosquitos de todos los tamaños. Los hay grandes, de esos gordos que molestan a la hora de comer, los hay chiquitos, de esos que no te dejan dormir. Incluso también los había puntiagudos, parecidos a aviones de guerra. Son insoportables.

He intentado de todo. Desde remedies caseros, hasta químicos horribles que estaban más cerca de matarme a mí que matar a los mosquitos. Gasté muchísimo dinero en esos medicamentos, e incluso tuve que pedir prestado dinero para poder lograrlo. Mi familia ya no me visita, porque detestan los mosquitos. Ya estoy harta.

Entro a un vivero, siguiendo el consejo de una amiga, tratando de encontrar algún tipo de árbol que los espante, alguna que desprenda algún olor especial que haga que se vayan y me liberen el hogar. Y, entre tantos árboles y flores de distintos colores, veo una que me llama la atención. Es muy verde, con una especie de dientes, y muy grande. Me enamoró a primera vista.

La llevo a casa, y hasta puedo sentir el miedo de los mosquitos al plantar a mi nueva amiga. Pequeña Boquita, la llamé. Y ayudó muchísimo con los invitados no deseados. A la semana, ya podía dormir tranquilamente. A los tres meses, ya podía dejar comida fuera de la heladera por más de cinco minutos que no pasaría nada. Y mi planta crecía y crecía y crecía. Ahora mide un metro y medio.

La veo en el patio, ya es más grande que yo. Muy verde, muy hermosa, muy grande. Veo una pequeña mosca gorda, una de esas que tanto me hizo la vida imposible durante tanto tiempo. La sigo con la mirada, y veo como se posa dentro de la boquita de mi planta. Me acerco mucho, quiero ver como se la come. Pequeña Boquita cierra su boca, todo se pone muy oscuro. Ya no recuerdo nada.

QUESTIONNAIRE

- What kind of plant do you think it is?
- Do you like mosquitoes?
- Have you ever been in a vivarium?
- Do you have any plants?
- Write short sentences about what kind of plants you have.

Let's review some grammar and fun facts!

For the ever-expanding list of "words with several translations" (that is the official title, but it's a bit long and not quite catchy):

Fly – volar ("Let's fly to Argentina!") or mosquito/mosca ("I hate this fly!")

Context is important, especially since in this case, we are talking about flying things.

TRANSLATION

My house is full of flies. It does not matter what time of the day or which season of the year we are talking about, there are always flies of every size. There are big ones, those fat ones that bother even at lunchtime, there are small ones, those that will not let you sleep at night. Even those that have pointy noses, which look like warplanes. They are unbearable.

I tried everything. From home remedies to horrible chemicals that were closer to killing me than killing the mosquitos. I spent a lot of money on those remedies and even had to borrow money in order to pay them. My family does not visit me anymore, because they hate mosquitos. I am fed up.

I went inside a vivarium, following a friend's advice, trying to find some kind of plant that scares them, any kind that gives off some special smell that makes them go away and free up my home. And, between so many trees and flowers of different colors, I saw one that catches my attention. It's very green, with some kind of teeth, and it was very big. I fell in love at first sight.

I took it home, and I could even feel the fear of the mosquitoes when I planted my new friend. Little Mouth, I name it. And it really helped with the unwanted guests. A week later, I could sleep peacefully. Three months later, I could leave food outside the fridge for more than five minutes and nothing would happen. And my plant grew and grew and grew. Now it is almost 5 feet tall.

I see it in the backyard, already bigger than me. Very green, very beautiful, very big. I see a small fat fly, one of those that made my life impossible for a long time. I follow it with my sight, and I see it pose down inside the mouth of my plant. I get closer, I want to see it how it eats it. Little Mouth closes its mouth. Everything gets dark. I can't remember anything.

"Amor a primera vista/Love at first sight"

El tren está lleno, es hora pico y todos nos dirigimos a nuestros trabajos. Apretados como si estuviéramos en una lata de sardinas. En medio de la gente, la veo. Ella, con su sonrisa reluciente. Ella, con ese pelo rubio hermoso. Ella, escuchando música y moviendo su cabeza. Y me enamoraste.

Llegamos a una de las estaciones principales, y la gente comienza a descender. Aprovecho para moverme desde donde estaba hacia donde estaba ella se encontraba. Quiero hablarle, quiero presentarme, quiero invitarla a salir. Pero justo cuando a punto de acercarme, mucha gente sube. Me dejan lejos de ella. Al menos mírame. Quiero sonreirte a la distancia. Mirame. Mirame. Mirame.

Girás y nuestras miradas se cruzan. Es en ese momento que te sonrío, y, por esas casualidades del destino, me devolvés la sonrisa. El mundo se me abre debajo de mis pies, y mi corazón salta ante la posibilidad de hablarte. Por supuesto, mi mente se vuelve loca con las posibilidades. Nos veo a nosotros yendo al cine, cenando en un restaurante caro, conociendo a nuestros padres, adoptando un perrito, comprando plantas, mudándonos a un hogar, discutiendo sobre quién cocina, felices porque conseguiste un trabajo nuevo, besándome porque te propuse matrimonio y dijiste que sí, casándonos, festejando, creciendo y envejeciendo juntos.

Te miro, y me pregunto si tendrás novio. Quizás tendrás ganas de conocer a alguien nuevo. ¿Y qué estarás estudiando? Yo diría que estás estudiando medicina o que estás tratando de recibirte de abogada. Miro, a la distancia, si tenés una mochila, o algo así, pero no puedo ver nada que me otorgue una pista de lo que te gusta, ni siquiera una pista de lo que es que te gusta. Qué comida te agrada. Qué es lo que amás hacer. Nada que me regale una idea de cuál es tu nombre.

Llegamos a otra estación, y recibiste una llamada de teléfono. No voy a escuchar lo que hablás, no soy esa clase de persona, pero escucho tu "Hola!" y me hacen cosquillas el estómago. Tenés una voz muy hermosa.

Ya está, me decido, voy a hablarte. Voy a preguntarte si para ir a tal lugar tengo que bajarme en la siguiente estación. Yo ya sé la respuesta, pero quiero hacerte algún chiste, quizás un poco de charla, algo que me deje hablarte un poco. Capaz hablarte del clima, o algo así.

Llegamos a una estación, y decidiste bajarte.

Te busco desde entonces.

No puedo encontrarte.

QUESTIONNAIRE

- Have you ever taken the subway during rush hour?
- Have you ever fallen in love at first sight?
- Write the perfect ending for you: Do they get together? Does she find him attractive?

Let's review some grammar and fun facts!

In English, you can say that you want to propose to your other half, and everybody will know what you mean. In Spanish, you have to say "propongo matrimonio" (propose marriage) because if you don't, you are just proposing and the speaker doesn't know what are you exactly proposing!

When you say "propongo" you might be saying that we could go out to eat, or to watch a movie, etc. You are proposing a plan, one that you might have to agree with the other person in the conversation.

There was a story about a man from Utah, or at least, that's what one of my closest friends once told me, who came to live in Chile, and had that exact same problem. Obviously, he didn't find it very funny but his girlfriend definitely did!

TRANSLATION

The train is full. It's rush hour and we are all going to work. Tight like we were inside a tuna can. In the midst of everyone, I see her. She, with her brilliant smile. She, with that beautiful blond hair. She, listening to music and moving her head. And you charmed me.

We get to one of the main stations, and people start descending. I use this to my advantage and start moving from where I was to where she is. I want to talk to her, I want to introduce myself, I want to ask her out. However, right when I was about to get close, a lot of people come in. They push me away from hee. At least look at me. I want to smile at you from a distance. Look at me. Look at me. Look at me.

You turned your head and we exchange looks. It is in that moment that I smile at you, and, by one of those casualties of destiny, you smile back. The world opens under my feet, and my heart jumps at the possibility of talking to you.

Of course, my mind goes crazy with the possibilities. I see us going to the theater, having dinner in an expensive restaurant, meeting our parents, adopting a little doggy, buying plants, moving to a new home, arguing about who cooks, happy because you got a new job, kissing me because I proposed to you and you said yes, getting married, celebrating, growing old together.

I look at you, and I wonder if you are dating someone. Maybe you want to meet someone new. And what are you studying? I would say that you are going to med school or that you are trying to graduate as a lawyer. I look, from the distance, if you have a backpack, or something like that, but I can't see anything that gives me a clue on what you like, nor even an idea on what it is that you love. What kind of food you like. What is it that you love to do. Nothing that gives me an idea on what your name is.

We arrive at another station, and you get a phone call. I'm not going to listen to your conversation, I'm not that kind of person, but I manage to listen to your "Hello!" and my stomach tickles. You have a very beautiful voice.

That's it, I am decided, I'm going to talk to you. I'm going to ask you if you wanted to go to whatever place I have to off in the next station. I already know the answer, but I want to make a joke, maybe a bit of small talk, something that allows me to talk to you for a bit. Maybe talk to you about the weather, or something like that.

We get to a station, and you decide to get off.

I've looked for you since.

I can't find you.

"El Extraño Libro / The Strange Book"

Encontré un libro en la biblioteca de mi abuelo. Era rojo, con letras doradas en la tapa, y en el lomo decía "Las Aventuras de Roberto" con letras negras y brillantes. Tenía una pequeña nota en la tapa.

No abrir

Bajo ninguna circunstancia, no abrir.

Mi curiosidad me ganó. Lo abrí. En la primera hoja encontré una nota escrita a mano, con la letra de mi abuelo.

Es tu última chance. No sigas. Desaparecerás.

Nunca fui bueno siguiendo las reglas y los pedidos, así que continué leyendo. La historia era bastante simple: Se trataba de un chico llamado Roberto, que vivía en una ciudad muy parecida a la mía. Estudiaba en un colegio, como el mío. También tenía un mejor amigo, justo igual que yo, y jugaba en el equipo de fútbol local, exactamente como yo.

Tenía el pelo rojo como el fuego, y la misma cara que la mía. Quien sea que haya escrito esto, era muy raro. Pero me encantaba seguir leyendo. En un momento, en la historia, Roberto entró en un hogar. Dentro, encontró cientos, miles de libros.

Hubo uno que le llamó la atención: "Las Aventuras de David". Me sorprendí que fuera mi nombre. Qué raro, pensé. Cuando llegué a la parte del texto donde lo abría, todo se me nubló y desaparecí dentro del libro.

Una figura me miraba fijamente, con el libro de Las Aventuras de David en las manos. Tenía una mirada profunda, penetrante.

Era yo.

Questionnaire

- What do you think happened?
- Have you ever read a book whose main character looked or acted just like you?
- What would you do if you find yourself inside a book?

Let's review some grammar and fun facts!

In Spanish, people say "dorsal" to refer to the book spine, because spine or thorn is "espina."

Be mindful of the context, like I always say.

Translation

I found a book in my grandfather's library. It was red, with golden letters in the front, and in the spine, it said, *The Adventures of Roberto* in black and shiny letters. It had a small note on the cover.

Don't open

Under no circumstance, don't open.

My curiosity won the best of me. I opened it. In the first page, I found a handwritten note, with my grandfather's handwriting.

It's your last chance. Don't proceed. You will be gone.

I was never good following orders and requests, so I kept reading. The story was very simple: It was about a kid named Roberto, who lived in a city very much like mine. Studied in a school, like mine. He also had a best friend, just like me, and played in the local football team, exactly like me.

He had red hair, like fire, and the same face, like me. Whoever had written this, it was very weird. But I loved to read it. One moment, during the story, Roberto entered a home. Inside, he found hundreds, thousands of books.

There was one that called his attention: *The Adventures of David.* I was surprised that it said my name. That's weird, I thought. When I got to the part where it opened, all went foggy and disappeared inside the book.

A figure stared deeply at me, with the *Adventures of David* book in his hands. He had a deep, penetrating gaze.

It was me.

"La máscara/The Mask"

La máscara cayó, se quebró y se deshizo en miles de pedazos. El terror se apoderó de mí. Era la máscara que usaba mamá cuando era joven para jugar con su padre, mi abuelo. Me la regaló cuando yo era muy chico. Era algo muy preciado para mí. Y ahora yacía en el suelo destrozada, y yo hice lo que pude para no ponerme a llorar.

Llevé los trozos a mi habitación, y tomé pegamento especial. Los apoyé en mi escritorio, encendí mi luz, y comencé a trabajar. Pedazo tras pedazo, los pegué de una manera muy cuidadosa. Tomé todos los recaudos para que nada estuviera fuera de lugar. Me tomó horas, toda una noche entera para poder terminar y dejarla como si fuera nueva. Limpié los restos de pegamento, y la dejé secar mientras yo me acostaba a descansar un poco.

En medio de la noche, me desperté asustado. Había sentido unos pequeños ruidos en el suelo de mi habitación, y era algo raro, ya que no tenía mascotas. Sonaba como si unas uñas se arrastraran por el suelo, y se dirigían hacia mi cama.

Encendí rápidamente la luz y pude ver una imagen fugaz de algo que se movía rápidamente hacia debajo de mi escritorio. Tomé mi linterna que se encontraba en mi mesa de luz, me acerqué y traté de investigar qué era lo que hacía ese ruido extraño. Desde debajo del escritorio, iluminado por mi linterna, pude ver que la máscara, cuyos ojos brillaban con un rojo profundo, me miraban fijamente. La boca, apenas pegada, se abrió, y cuando habló, la voz la sentí dentro de mí. Me pidió que la tomara, y que la usara.

No pude evitarlo.

Estiré mi brazo, la tomé y me la apoyé en la cara. Inmediatamente, desaparecí en una nube. Desperté en una especie de ciudad futurista, donde había seres que tenían en la cara máscaras parecidas a la mía. Se comunicaban con su mente, o al menos, así lo sentía. Sus ciudades eran gigantes, enormes, con varias civilizaciones bajo su dominio. Se habían extendido por las estrellas, y tenían el control sobre las emociones. Caminé por la ciudad, usando el cuerpo que me otorgaba la máscara. En ellas, vi desolación, y vi también locura.

Entré a un edificio que parecía un museo. Tenían expuesto, o al menos así parecía, seres de formas que no entendía, cubos y triángulos con aspecto extraño que flotaban en una especie de líquido que hacía que estuvieran suspendidos en el aire. También podía ver que tenían fragmentos de otros planetas, y de algunos soles.

Seguí caminando, y pude ver carteles con letras extrañas, y lo que parecía ser como automóviles volando en el aire, con muchos de estas máscaras caminando por ahí. No parecía como que las máscaras habían construido esto, sino más bien, habían tomado el control del lugar, quizás tomando posesión de los seres que ya vivían acá. Cuando veo que mi cuerpo me llevaba a algunos barrios, pude notar que había seres que no tenían la máscara, y que tenían marcas en la cara como si la hubieran tenido hace tiempo. Era extraño. Mi cuerpo no me dejó ver más sobre esto, y me llevó al sector donde estarían los infantes.

Ahí estaban en filas, en lo que parecía un colegio, estudiando sobre civilizaciones, estrellas largamente perdidas, y todos, todos de ellos, con la mirada de la máscara encima de sus caras. Caras perdidas, y atentas. Era espeluznante. Comencé a tener muchísimo miedo. Pude reconocer en una placa que parecía ser un pizarrón un sistema solar parecido al nuestro, como se lo mostraría desde el espacio.

El cuerpo me llevó hacia otro sector, el lugar donde estaban los avances científicos. Eran edificios altos, de color blanco, donde se podía ver que experimentaban sobre armas y naves de distintos tamaños. Tenían el conocimiento, o al menos eso me parecía, de poder experimentar con agujeros negros, o la materia en sí misma. Entré en una de las habitaciones más grandes, siempre llevado por el cuerpo que me otorgaba la máscara.

Vi como esa civilización estaba investigando sobre viajes en el tiempo, y cómo, uno de esos seres se subía a una máquina, y desaparecía en el espacio. De alguna manera, supe que la máscara le había informado a los otros seres que nosotros no estábamos listos. Que prepararan las armas mentales, que cuando llegaran, no podríamos hacer nada.

También vi como esa nave caía en la Tierra, hace muchísimos años. Vi como mi Abuelo tomaba la máscara, sin saber su origen. Vi los juegos de mi madre con esa máscara. Y vi, no, sentí el dolor absoluto cuando se cayó al suelo hoy y se partió.

Me saqué la máscara, respiré profundo, tomé un martillo, y la destrocé a golpes.

Espero que con esto sea suficiente.

QUESTIONNAIRE

- What would you do if you find an old mask?
- Write ten sentences that expand the world of the mask.

Let's review some grammar and fun facts!

In this story, we don't have many new words, and none of the words that might have several meanings. But one example might be that "mask" might apply to a mask like in the story (or in the Jim Carrey comedy movie).

TRANSLATION

The mask fell, broke and tore into thousands of pieces. The terror took over me. It was the mask that my mother used to play with her father, my grandfather. She gave it to me when I was really young. It was something really precious for me. And now it lay on the floor smashed, and I did what I could to not start to cry.

I took the pieces to my room and grabbed special glue. I left them on my desk, turned on my light, and started to work. Piece by piece, I glued it together in a very careful manner. I took all the precautions necessary to avoid anything to be out of place. It takes me hours, and an entire night to finish it and leave it like new. I cleaned up the glue residue and left it to dry while I laid down to get some rest.

In the middle of the night, I woke up scared. I had heard some small noises on the floor of my bedroom, and it was weird since I did not have any pets. It sounded like if some nails dragged on the floor, and approaching my bed.

I quickly turned on the light and I caught a glimpse of something that went quickly under my desk. I grabbed the flashlight that I had in my night table, got closer and tried to investigate what was doing that strange noise.

From under my desk, illuminated by my flashlight, I could see that the mask, whose eyes were shining with a deep red, stared at me deeply. The mouth, barely glued together, opened up, and when it spoke, I felt the voice inside me. It asked me to take it and use it.

I couldn't help myself.

I stretched out my arm, took it and put it on my face. Immediately, I disappeared in a cloud. I woke up in some sort of futuristic city, where there were beings that had masks like mine on their faces.

They communicated with each other using their minds, or, at least, that's how I felt it. Their cities were gigantic, huge, with several civilizations under their rule. They had extended over the stars, and had control over emotions. I walked all over the city, using the body that the mask gave me. In it, I saw desolation, and I also saw madness.

I walked inside a building that looked like a museum. They were showing, or at least that is what it looked like, beings of a shape that I couldn't understand, cubes and triangles with a strange look that were floating in some sort of liquid that forced them to be suspended in the air. I could also see that they had fragments of different planets, and from some suns.

I kept walking, and I could see billboards with strange letters, and what looked like automobiles flying in the air, with several of these masks walking around there. It didn't look like the masks had built this, but, more like they had taken over the place, maybe taking possession of the beings that were already living in here. When I see that my body took me to different neighborhoods, I notice that there were several beings that didn't have masks, and had marks on their faces like they already had it long ago. It was strange. My body didn't let me see more of this, and took me to the place where the kids would were.

There they were in rows, in what looked like a school, studying about civilizations, stars long forgotten, and all, all of them, with the look of the mask all over their faces. Lost faces, and staring. It was creepy. I started to be very afraid. I could recognize in a plaque that looked like a blackboard a solar system like ours, like one might look at it from space.

The body took me to another sector, the place where the scientific advances were. There were tall buildings, colored white, where one could see that they were experimenting with weapons and ships of different sizes. They had the knowledge, or at least that was what it looked like to me, of being able to experiment over black holes, or the matter itself. I walked inside one of the largest rooms, always carried by the body that the masks allowed me to have.

I saw how that civilization was researching on time travel, and how, one of those beings went into a machine and disappeared in space. Somehow, I knew that the mask had informed the other beings that we weren't ready. That they had to prepare the mental weapons, that when they arrive, there was nothing we could do.

I also saw how that ship fell into Earth, a long time ago. I saw how my Grandfather took the mask, without knowing its origin. I saw my mother playing with that mask. And I saw, no, I felt the absolute pain when it fell down and broke in pieces.

I took off the mask, took a deep breath, grabbed a hammer and smashed into pieces.

I hope that this is enough.

"El amor de mi vida/The love of my life"

La motocicleta me llevó por toda la ciudad. Era mi vieja amiga. El ruido del motor era muy suave, casi como terciopelo. La compré hace 10 años, y desde entonces que me acompaña a todos lados. La llevé en el primer día de mi trabajo, esquivamos tormentas juntos, me ayudó a conquistar chicas (y conocer a mi actual esposa), e incluso, pude rescatarla cuando la robaron. Recuerdo ese día: Salí de la oficina a las 4 de la tarde, como es usual, y cuando miro hacia donde la había dejado en el estacionamiento, ya no estaba.

Llamé a la policía, puse carteles por todos lados, investigué en los sitios de venta de motocicletas usadas, porque quizás alguien la quería vender. A esta altura, ya no quería justicia, quería a mi motocicleta de vuelta conmigo.

Pasaron 3 meses, y yo seguía sin mi moto. A la noche la extrañaba. Cuando tenía que ir a trabajar, mi primer instinto era ir a mi garaje, ponerme el casco y subirme. Durante esos tres meses, todos los días, sin falta, hacía la misma rutina. Mi motocicleta no podía estar sin mí. Necesitaba mis caricias, mis palabras de cariño. Solíamos charlar cuando volvía del trabajo, donde le contaba todo lo que me sucedía. Incluso, cuando tenía días depresivos, mi mejor remedio era subirme y simplemente andar. Mi motocicleta me entendía, y me contestaba con pequeños rugidos del motor para alegrarme, o contestarme una pregunta.

La necesitaba. Por eso no me sorprendí cuando un jueves, exactamente tres meses desde que la habían robado, abrí la puerta del garaje, y sentí un pequeño ruido familiar. Se me llenaron los ojos de lágrimas. Corrí a abrazarla, y puedo jurarles, aunque sé que no me van a creer, que la moto también estaba llorando. Su pequeño motor me hacía ronroneo. Inmediatamente la revisé, me fijé que no le faltara nada. Alguna que otra marca, mucho barro, y varias marcas de cigarrillo que me enfurecían. ¿Cómo puede ser que no te hayan cuidado, hermano? Llamé a mi trabajo, me pedí mis vacaciones debido a una emergencia familiar, y me encerré en casa a repararla. Mientras, le contaba todo lo que se había perdido en este tiempo, y mi esposa, fiel y comprensiva, me miraba con una sonrisa enorme. No quiso ayudarme, simplemente saludó a mi moto, y nos dejó solos. Sabía que era algo privado, algo que nos conectaba a los dos.

Luego de varias horas, y con la pintura ya seca y lista para ser estrenada, decidí dar una vuelta. Me subí, me puse el casco, y arranqué.

Cuánto te extrañé, mi querida moto.

No voy a dejar que te vuelva a pasar algo nunca más.

QUESTIONNAIRE

- Have you ever ridden on a bicycle?
- What about a motorcycle?
- Try to write, in five sentences, the point of view from the bike.

Let's review some grammar and fun facts!

We keep adding words that have several translations (at this point, we could write a book about it!). Here's an important example that might help you on a daily basis:

In English, we say bike to refer to two different kinds of transports. In Spanish, those are two words separately:

Bicicleta: the one that Lance Armstrong used

Motocicleta/Moto: a bike with two wheels and an engine. For example, a Honda, Suzuki, etc).

And while we are on the subject of motorcycles, the Harley Davidson bikes that you might have seen in movies or TV shows are called choppers, and in Spanish, there is a word that derives from the original English one: choperas.

But, and here's the fun thing, there's also a size of glass that is named choperas. In English, it's a beer mug. In Spanish, they use choperas. It's a big large glass that is often served really cold and kept in the freezer, and only used when you open a new bottle of beer.

You won't find that kind of glass for wine or water, though. Those are specifically for alcoholic beverages.

TRANSLATION

The motorcycle took me all over the city. It was my old friend. The sound of the engine was really soft, almost like velvet. I bought it 10 years ago, and since then it has gone with me everywhere. I took it on the first day of my job, avoided storms together, it helped me to seduce girls (and meet my actual wife), and, I even rescued it when it was stolen.

I remember that day: I left the office at four in the afternoon, like usual, and when I looked where I had left it in the parking lot, it wasn't there anymore.

I called the cops, posted signs everywhere; I looked on every used bike website because maybe someone wanted to sell it. At this point, I didn't want justice, I just wanted my bike with me again.

Three months passed, and I was still without my bike. I missed it at night. When I had to go to work, my first instinct was to go to my garage, put on my helmet and hop on. During all those three months, every day, without missing a day, I did the same routine.

My bike couldn't be without me. It needed my caresses, my words of love. We used to talk while I got back from work, where I told it everything that happened to me. Even, when I had depressing days, my best remedy was to get on and just ride. My bike understood me and answered me with small growls from the engine to cheer me up, or to answer a question.

I needed it. That's why I wasn't surprised when a Thursday, exactly three months after it had been stolen, I opened up my garage door, and I heard a small familiar noise.

My eyes were full of tears. I went to hug it, and I can swear, even though I know that you are not going to believe me, that the bike was also crying.

Its small engine purred at me. Immediately, I examined it, checking out to see that nothing was missing. It had some marks, a lot of mud and several cigarettes marks that got me really angry. How could it be that they hadn't taken care of you, man?

I called work, I asked for leave due to a family emergency, and locked up at home to repair it. Meanwhile, I told it everything that it had missed during all this time, and my wife, loyal and understanding, watched me with a huge smile on her face. She didn't want to help me; she just waved to my bike and left us alone. She knew it was something private, something that connected us both.

After several hours, and with the paint already dry and the bike ready to be ridden again, I decided to go for a spin. I hopped on, put on my helmet, and started it.

How much I missed you, my dear bike.

I won't let anything happen to you anymore.

"¿Inocente o culpable?/Innocent or guilty?"

Voy a serles enteramente honesto: Existe la posibilidad de que yo sea el causante de la Tercera Guerra Mundial. Antes que se enojen conmigo, déjenme explicarles.

Estaba aburrido en casa, sin nada que hacer, cuando decidí divertirme. Mi conexión a Internet no funcionaba, y mi computadora no era tan rápida y moderna como para poder instalar algún juego moderno, y la verdad es que ya me había aburrido de leer los textos para el colegio. Eran muy aburridos, y además, no iba a ir al colegio durante dos semanas porque estaba en vacaciones de invierno. Entonces, recordé algo que me había comentado mi padre una vez hace mucho tiempo: que cuando él era joven, se divertían jugando en el patio, o haciendo llamadas de broma.

Bueno, afuera llovía mucho, así que eso ya estaba descartado. Pero la idea de las llamadas broma me encantaba. Tomé la guía telefónica, y marqué el primer número que encontré. Me atendió un señor grande.

> Hola

> Eh, sí, hola. Mi nombre es… - Tuve que improvisar – David, y quería saber si cuando abre la canilla, sale agua.

> A ver, un momento – No podía creerlo, el señor realmente fue a revisar. Esto no tenía sentido – Sí, está saliendo agua. ¿Por qué lo pregunta?

La risa me ganó. No pude continuar. El señor me dijo varias cosas que, por respeto a todos ustedes, no voy a repetir. Estuve toda la tarde haciéndolo, primero marcando números de la guía telefónica, y ya al final, cuando me estaba aburriendo, números al azar. Ahí fue cuando, en una de esas llamadas, me atendió una voz rasposa y robótica

> ¿Contraseña?

> Eh… Cuando abre la canilla, ¿sale agua?

Un silencio del otro lado de la línea.

> Contraseña aceptada.

Y la línea murió. Esto sucedió el… diez de enero. Y todos sabemos qué pasó el día siguiente, ¿verdad?

> *Señor, le pedimos que, a efectos de claridad, explique qué sucedió al día siguiente.*

Está bien, su Señoría. Al día siguiente, Rusia (o al menos, en ese entonces se llamaba Rusia) cerró sus fronteras, y lo que luego sería conocido como la Liga de las Naciones Nucleares lanzó sus misiles nucleares, comenzando una lluvia de destrucción sobre todo lo que tocaban.

> *Está bien. Hemos oído todo lo que necesitábamos oír.*

> *¿Cómo se declara el acusado?*

Inocente, su Señoría. Yo no sabía que mi broma iba a terminar generando semejante desastre. Ni menos pensé que la Humanidad se encontraría al borde de la destrucción. De hecho, yo no disparé los misiles, ni tampoco ordené a los ejércitos luchar, así que, técnicamente hablando, yo soy inocente.

Esta Corte encuentra al acusado culpable. Se lo condena a trabajo forzado en las prisiones atómicas de la Luna. Se levanta la sesión.

QUESTIONNAIRE

- Have you ever made a prank call? Answer in Spanish.
- What was the prank call? Did your victim get mad?
- Let's say you find yourself in a situation just like the main character: Would you say that you are guilty, or innocent?
- What do you think happened on the Moon? What are your thoughts on it?
- Write a different ending where he is found not guilty. Try to get into the character and what he would do in that situation.

Let's review some grammar and fun facts!

The basis of the joke is something an old friend once told me that he used to do it when he was a kid, but the ending is a bit reworked. The original prank included an answer that it was something in the vein of, "Well, what would you expect to come out? Wine?"

That was taken from an old comedy show that was really famous on TV during the 60s, and then expanded into the rest of the continent.

What is funny is that while writing this, I actually got a prank call from some kids, but instead of innocently asking me about my water, they asked me if my fridge was working. Needless to say, I did check out if my fridge was working correctly. The laugh that I heard from this side of the line was too much, and I had to laugh with them.

In the grammar side of the story, in Spanish, dates are written like this:

14 de Febrero

10 de Enero

31 de Diciembre

Putting the day first, and then the month. In English, it's backwards. That brings several problems with the date format. In the USA and some parts of Europe, the day is written MM/DD/YYYY (months, days, and years), but in Spanish, it is written DD/MM/YYYY (days, months, and years).

Here's a handy guide of the name of the months and their respective translation:

January - Enero

February - Febrero

March - Marzo

April - Abril

May - Mayo

June - Junio

July - Julio

August - Agosto

September – Septiembre (some places write it as Setiembre, without the p. That's because the pronunciation of the p in Septiembre is hard for some dialects.

October - Octubre

November - Noviembre

December – Diciembre

TRANSLATION

I'm going to be entirely honest with you: There exists the possibility that I might have caused World War III. Before you get angry with me, allow me to explain.

I was bored at home, without anything to do, when I decided to have some fun. My internet connection didn't work, and my computer wasn't as fast and modern so I could install any recent game, and the truth is that I got bored of reading the books for school. They were very boring, and besides, I wasn't going to go to the school for two weeks since I was in my winter holidays.

Then I remembered something that my father once told me a long time ago: That when he was young, he had fun playing in the backyard, or making prank calls.

Well, it was raining a lot outside, so the backyard was out of the question. But I loved the idea of prank calls. I took out the phone guide and dialled the first number that I found. It answered an old man.

> "Hello."

> "Eh, yeah, hello. My name is…" - I had to improvise – "David, and I wanted to check that when you turn on your faucet, water comes out."

> "Let me see. One moment." I couldn't believe it, the guy actually went to check it out.

> "This didn't make sense. Yeah, water is coming out. Why do you ask?"

Laughter overcame me. I couldn't continue. The mister told me several things that, out of respect to all of you, I won't repeat. I spent all afternoon doing it, first dialing numbers from the phone book, and at the end, when I was getting bored, random numbers. That's when, during one of those calls, it answered a raspy and robotic voice

> "Password?"

> "Eh… When you turn on the faucet, does wáter come out?"

Silence from the other side of the line.

"Password accepted."

And the line went dead. That happened on… January the tenth. And we all know what happened next day, right?

Sir, we ask you to, for the purpose of clarification, explain what happened the next day.

All right, your Honor. Next day, Russia (or at least, during that time it was named Rusia) closed up their borders, and what was later to be known as the Nuclear League of Nations launched their nuclear missiles, starting a rain of destruction over everything they touched.

All right. We heard everything that we needed to hear.

How does the defendant plead?

Not guilty, your Honor. I didn't know that my joke was going to start such a mess. And I didn't think that humankind was going to be at the edge of destruction. In fact, I didn't shoot the missiles, nor did I ordered the militaries to fight, so, technically speaking, I am innocent.

This Court finds the defendant guilty. He is sentenced to forced labor in the atomic jails on the Moon. Court dismissed.

"Vuelve/Come back"

Veo el resto de comida que dejaste en la mesa. Te extraño. No te vayas. Quiero abrazarte nuevamente. Quiero que te quedes, al menos una noche más.

Perdón. Es mi culpa. Te pido disculpas. No debí gritarte. Volvé. Quiero que nos acostemos los dos, y te acaricie la cabeza mientras vemos alguna película. Quiero que te quedes conmigo. Puedo cocinarte la comida que quieras. No me dejes.

Volvé, pequeño gatito.

QUESTIONNAIRE

- What were you thinking the story was about before reading the twist ending?
- Have you ever gotten a pet? A cat, fish or a dog?
- Take a blank page, and write down a story about that pet. If you never had one, imagine one.
- Try to do it in Spanish.

Let's review some grammar and fun facts!

My stories almost always involve pets because I love them. I grew up with several cats and kittens, and I can't avoid writing about them.

On the grammar side of the (really short) story, scratch can be translated both as "rascar" ("Scratch my head, please") and "rayar" ("This window is scratched").

One of the fun and interesting things is that in South America, they use a lot of English words that aren't translated, and part of the normal and usual conversation. For example, a DJ scratches a vinyl when he is making some music, right? Well, in Spanish, they don't say "rayar el disco," they just say, "Ese DJ scratcheó el disco!" (That DJ scratched the disk!)

TRANSLATION

I see the leftovers that you left on the table. I miss you. Don't go. I want to hug you again. I want you to stay, at least one more night.

I'm sorry. It is my fault. I apologize. I shouldn't have screamed at you. I want us to lie down, and I'd scratch your head while we watch a movie. I want you to stay with me. I can cook any food that you want. Don't leave me.

Come back, little kitten.

"El Bailarín que Salvó al Mundo/The dancer who saved the World"

La invasión fue fácil de detener. De hecho, tan fácil, que muchos dirían que casi fue una mentira. Verán, un día la Humanidad se despertó y se dio cuenta que no estaba sola en el Universo. Sí, es cierto, habíamos encontrado bacterias, e indicios de vida en Marte y Neptuno, pero nada que sea remotamente parecido a vida inteligente.

Un día nos despertamos, y todos los seres humanos notaron que tenían un ser verde, con pequeños cuernitos, flotando cerca de ellos. En todas partes del mundo, los reportes sobre la aparición misteriosa de estos seres llenaron las tapas de los diarios, y el terror tomó varias víctimas a lo largo del planeta.

Fue horrible. Varios meses de desastres, y caos, hasta que al poco tiempo nos dimos cuenta que esos seres, quienes sean que sea, no nos hacían nada. De hecho, ni siquiera tenían ojos ni oídos, o al menos nada parecido a eso. Simplemente flotaban alrededor nuestro. Algunas personas, incluso, comenzaron a adoptarlas como mascotas. Y al poco tiempo, como muchas otras veces en la historia de la Humanidad, nos acostumbramos y seguimos con nuestras vidas. Básicamente, continuamos peleando, siendo egoístas, luchando el uno contra el otro por las cosas más menores.

Llegó el punto en el que esos seres, apodados Marcianitos (aunque no sabíamos si siquiera si venían de Marte o de alguna otra galaxia), fueron tan parte de la vida cotidiana, que incluso comenzaron a tener programas de televisión, videojuegos, películas, investigaciones científicas, libros escritos al respecto. De hecho, también se pudo verificar que alrededor de cada persona, luego de la aparición de los Marcianitos, comenzaba a aparecer un aura verde, del mismo tono que el ser extraño. Se pudo verificar rápidamente cuando se revisaron estudios antiguos, y luego, estudios hechos nuevamente. Es como si eso seres realmente sí tenían un efecto entre nosotros.

Y un día, apareció una persona que dijo que sabía cómo eliminarlos. Bueno, no fue la primera. Desde la aparición de los Marcianitos, hubo cientos de personas que ofrecían curas mágicas para solucionarlo, desde meditación hasta pastillas, todo por una módica suma, obvio.

Pero esta persona decía que desde que hizo un baile, se fue su Marcianito. Al principio nadie le creía, pero cuando se le hicieron estudios, se pudo notar que realmente había un cambio en su persona. Por supuesto, al principio se lo trató como fraude, pero la realidad es que él no quería fama, ni tampoco solicitaba dinero (a diferencia de las otras personas que ofrecían curas), y de hecho, sólo ofreció su ayuda porque la gente de su pueblo se lo pidió. Así que al que lo deseaba, podía aprender su baile, totalmente gratis, y enseñarle a otros para que pudieran lograrlo.

Su baile era extraño. No tenía forma, y ni siquiera parecía una coreografía bien pensada. Era más bien mover los brazos y las piernas de manera aleatoria, y listo. No había razón, ni estilo, ni gracia. Él decía que lo había descubierto cuando estaba tratando de aprender un nuevo estilo de baile para el que realmente no servía, y en su frustración, movió las piernas y brazos muy enojado. Y así fue como su Marcianito se fue.

Cientos de personas lo intentaron, grabaron videos y lo compartieron en todas las redes sociales. Miles de personas lo copiaron, logrando que todos sus Marcianitos desaparecieran. Se organizaron festivales de baile y de despedida a los Marcianitos, donde la gente se juntaba, comía, y bailaban. Al poco tiempo, esto llevó a un buen acercamiento entre la gente, que a su vez llevó a entendimientos entre ciudades, luego países, y así, sin disparar un solo tiro, comenzaron a desaparecer las guerras, y de a poco, se pudo ir trabajando por un futuro mejor.

Era raro de pensar, pero los Marcianitos y su posterior derrota nos habían cambiado de una manera fundamental, mostrándonos que no sólo no estábamos solos, sino que además, era demasiado inútil seguir combatiendo.

Esta forma de pensar nos llevó a las estrellas, y luego, hacia otras dimensiones. Establecimos contacto con miles de especies, y formamos alianzas. La humanidad creció a pasos agigantados, siempre siguiendo el ejemplo de ese bailarín extraño, que en su frustración, nos demostró que podemos ser mejores.

Y esta es la historia de cómo un bailarín salvó al mundo.

QUESTIONNAIRE

- What were the creatures like?
- What was the dance like? Have you ever tried it?
- In short sentences, try to rework the ending. But here's a catch: Try to do it in Spanish.

TRANSLATION

The invasion was easy to stop. In fact, so easy, that many might say that it was almost a lie. You see, one day, humanity woke up and realized that it wasn't alone in the Universe. Yeah, it's true; we had found bacteria and some signs of life on Mars and Neptune, but nothing that was remotely similar to intelligent life.

One day we woke up, and every human being noticed that they had a green being, with small horns, floating near them. In every part of the world, the reports over the mysterious apparition of these beings filled up the newspaper pages, and the terror took many victims across the planet.

It was horrible. Several months of disasters and chaos, until a bit later we realized that those beings, whoever they were, didn't do anything to us. In fact, they didn't even have eyes or ears, or at least nothing resembling that. They just floated around us. Some people, even, started adapting them as pets. And soon after that, like many other times in the history of Mankind, we got used to it and continued with our lives. Basically, we continued to fight, being selfish, arguing against each other for the most trivial things.

It came to the point that those beings, nicknamed Little Martians (although we didn't even know if they came from Mars or from another galaxy), were so integrated in our daily life, that we even started to have television shows, video games, movies, scientific research, books written about them.

In fact, we could also verify that each person, after the apparition of the Little Martians, started to show a green aura, the same tone of the strange being. It could be quickly checked when they checked out old studies, and then, the same studies done recently. It's like these beings had an effect over us.

And one day, someone said he knew how to eliminate them. Well, it wasn't the first one. From the first appearance of the Little Martians, there were hundreds of people that offered magical cures to fix it, from meditation to pills, all for a small fee, of course.

But this person said since he did his dance, his Little Martian went away. At first, nobody believed him, but when research took place, it could be noted that there was really a change in him. Of course, at first it was treated as fraud, but the reality is that he didn't want any fame, nor asked for money (unlike all other people who offered cures), and in fact, just offered his help because the people of his town asked him to. So to whoever wished for it, they could learn his dance, completely free of charge, and show other people to teach them to do it.

His dance was strange. It didn't have any shape, and it didn't even look like a well-thought choreography. It was more moving the arms and the legs in a random way, and that's it. It didn't have any reason, nor style, nor grace. He said that he found out when he was trying to learn a new dancing style for which he really wasn't good enough, and in his frustration, moved his legs and arms in anger. And that's how his Little Martian went away.

Hundreds of people tried, they recorded videos and shared it on all social media. Thousands of people copied it, making their Little Martian disappear. Dance and Little Martian goodbye festivals were organized where people gathered to eat and dance. Soon after that, this made people got really close, which in turn led to a really close understanding between cities, and then countries, and just like that, without shooting a single bullet, wars started to disappear, and bit by bit, everyone could start working on a better future.

It was weird to think about it, but the Little Martians and their ulterior defeat had changed us in a fundamental way, not just showing us that we were not alone, but that it was also pointless to keep fighting.

This way of thinking took us to the stars, and then, to other dimensions. We established contact with thousands of species, and alliances were forged. Humankind grew up in gigantic steps, always following the example of that strange dancer, who, in his frustration, showed us that we could be better.

And that's the story about how a dancer saved the world.